Real Life. Real God. Real Hope!

Devotions Inspiring a Jesus-view of Reality

Shelli Prindle

PRESS

Real Life. Real God. Real Hope!
Devotions Inspiring a Jesus-View of Reality
by Shelli Prindle

Printed in the United States of America

ISBN 9781612159034

www.xulonpress.com

To my dear nephews, Noah and Jake,
who hold my heart forever and bring me deepest joy;
may you trust Jesus always.

In Praise of
Real Life. Real God. Real Hope!

In Jesus Christ, God has provided to us a Savior that makes possible for joy to be a part of everyday life. *Real Life. Real God. Real Hope!* offers the soul a refreshing drink into the reality and truth of God's Word and its intersection with everyday life. Shelli Prindle insightfully uncovers the precious truths of scriptures while at the same time offers practical application for all who are on the journey of life - and who daily look for hope. Thank you, Shelli, for your devoted love for God's Word and for making it your passion to proclaim the message of the Psalmist, "Your Word has given me life."

Dr. David Hegedus
Associate Director
Association of Christian Schools International
Northeast Region

I know few people who have such an absolute passion for the Word of God. Shelli's ability to dig deeply into Scripture and find the truths that are revealed there is exceptional – God truly reveals Himself to her in a special way. She shares these nuggets of truth from the Lord with a contagious joy, and God in turn uses her wisdom and joy to change your life.

Shelli is a person of integrity, honor and true godliness. Her passion is not only for the Word of God but for people. She wants everyone she meets to fully embrace a personal relationship with

Jesus. As an educator, leader and speaker, Shelli has lived her life using her talents, struggles, joys and pains to shape her heart so that it beats for the things of God and Heaven.

As a woman who serves in full-time ministry, I am inspired by people who make a great and godly impact on my life and in the world around me - making a difference for eternity. Shelli Prindle is surely one of those people. I know that God will use these devotions to help you understand Him in a deeper and more personal way.

Jennifer Marsalese
Children's Ministry Director
Cornerstone Ministries
Export, PA

Acknowledgements

God has blessed me to be surrounded with wonderful, giving people. I wish to thank a few integral ones who helped make this book a reality:

Karen Fulton faithfully administrates and does all the invaluable behind-the-scenes work that makes Hope & Passion Ministries possible. Her peaceful, servant's heart is essential to my efforts. There would be no book without her endless contribution in ways innumerable. Her Christ-centered friendship is a blessing most unbelievable, and one for which I am grateful every day.

The Christian school faculty and staff I have been privileged to serve were my encouraging sounding board, a live audience for the birth of many of these devotions.

Wendy Knepp provided priceless technical and graphic design help to this ministry.

The board of directors of Hope & Passion Ministries has sacrificed time and prayed faithfully for the will of God to be done. I am very grateful to Kelsey Burger, Karen Fulton, Reverend James Henigen, Bobbi Latshaw, Yvonne Simmons, and Richard Termin.

My parents, Richard and Kay Termin, raised me to stand strong in the Lord, no matter what happens.

My husband, Jeff, has faithfully and patiently supported me in all ways, making the ministry to which God has called me possible.

Above all, my Savior, Jesus Christ, has redeemed my life from the pit and given me hope I do not deserve. Without Him, I am lost. Thank You, Jesus, for saving me and keeping me and allowing me to glorify You in my life. Thank You, also, for the reality of Heaven.

With a Single Breath

I know that You can do all things, and that no purpose of Yours can be thwarted.

Job 42:2

A pesky cold, a serious disease, an overheated engine, a family crisis, a preparation oversight, someone else's mistake, my own failure, a selfish plot, a jealous scheme, even death – all of these are just some of the things that can thwart the best of human plans. In an instant, the best of intentions can be brought to nothing.

How diametrically different are the eternal plans of God Almighty! Not one iota of a single plan of God can ever be stopped. Not one. For God, there are no unexpected illnesses, no mechanical failures, no tragedies, no storms, no lack of preparation, no episodes of exhaustion, no encounters with death, and no human sins that could ever challenge His power. With a single breath, He can blow any circumstance in the direction that fulfills His plan.

Amazingly, the man we most often identify as one who suffered the widest range of human tragedy, Job, said of His Lord, "I know that You can do all things, and that no purpose of Yours can be thwarted" (Job 42:2).

For those of us who posit the existence of the God of the Bible, we must also acknowledge His ability to accomplish exactly what He wills; for the God of the Bible is all-powerful, present everywhere, and all-knowing. As the Creator, He stands infinitely far above His creation. Not even willful, human rebellion against Him ever stood a chance; commanding natural things do His bidding without question, God Himself came down to earth and suffered His own wrath as the cure for sin.

God can do all things. Hear those words, "God can do all things." He can take every single moment of time – and every single circumstance of the combined lives of all people – and command

11

these moments and these circumstances to stand at attention and accomplish His ultimate design.

So, let them come. Let the surprising, disappointing, maddening, ridiculous, heartbreaking, and gravely annoying circumstances of life come. *No plan of God's will be thwarted*.

My responsibility is to be sure – unmistakably sure – that my plans are wrapped in the plans of God. "Lord, let me think your thoughts, abide by your Word, have your heart, renounce all pride, and keep my eyes fixed on You; for anything I plan outside of You will be stopped. But, *Your* plans go on into eternity completely unscathed. Amen."

From Messy to Glory

For you died, and your life is now hidden with Christ in God. When Christ, who is your life, appears, then you will also appear with him in glory.

Colossians 3:3-4 (NIV)

We are familiar with the beauty of the adult monarch butterfly. The orange and black pattern of the delicate wings reminds us of life's small miracles. We know the butterfly was once a caterpillar. The crawling insect became a thing of grace that sails in the air around us.

Do you realize the caterpillar started as a tiny egg about the size of the period at the end of a sentence? And do you further realize that the bright little caterpillar shed its final layer of skin to become a chrysalis? The green chrysalis is not a cocoon, but rather the actual body of the monarch caterpillar.

Truly amazing is what happens to the chrysalis while hanging on a silk pad. The caterpillar body's own digestive juices eat away the caterpillar tissue. The whole thing breaks down into a rich culture medium, or – put simply – mush! Then a miraculous process takes place in that mysterious liquid as imaginal cells begin to form the parts of the new, butterfly body. Cells in that mush direct what used to be a caterpillar to now grow wings! Soon the fluid media begins to transform into a butterfly. What a process! The caterpillar turns to liquid in the chrysalis, and the liquid turns to butterfly.

Now, if we were to interrupt the process and try to peek inside the chrysalis too soon, we would see what appears to be a gooey mess. In fact, a class of first grade students I know observed this very thing when a caterpillar bit a hole in a chrysalis. The liquid came out of the chrysalis, and the soon-to-be butterfly was destroyed. Sure, the process is somewhat messy when the chrysalis is young, but the splendor is just around the corner.

When it comes time for the monarch butterfly to emerge with its newly transformed body, the chrysalis undergoes a stunning change – it becomes clear. The green turns translucent when the gorgeous butterfly is about to appear.

God is demonstrating glorious truths in the metamorphosis of the monarch butterfly. First, the work of the Lord in a person's life can at times appear messy. The goo of the chrysalis may not seem attractive, but God works miracles in that goo! The cells He has placed in the liquid are working their way into a butterfly. In the same way, our lives – and the lives of fellow Christians – may not always seem as they ought. But, God is working miracles in the mess!

Second, there exists a certain mystery to who we truly are in Christ. For now, we struggle with sin in a broken world, and the truth of our being may not always be clear. Just like the green of the chrysalis in the beginning stages, God is yet working His plan in this age of grace. However, when Jesus comes back, we will appear with Him in glory! The real me will then be seen. The heart that has been cleansed by the blood of Jesus will be truly set free in that New Heavens and New Earth to be as He is. Just as the glory of Jesus is not completely revealed until the splendor of His Second Coming, so the glory of His followers is not yet visible. It will be, though. Without a doubt, when Jesus appears in all His glory, we will appear as we ought!

Do not give up, do not be discouraged, and do not give in. Let the goo of the chrysalis remind you of the beauty of the butterfly. We will be free!

Burst of Brilliance at the Death of Me

That which you sow does not come to life unless it dies. . .
I Corinthians 15:36

The radiance of autumn leaves
In all their warm grandeur
Strikes at the core of me.

What a burst of brilliance
Comes rushing to the scene
As the air grows cold.

Reds and oranges and yellows
Demanding to be admired;
We are drawn to their glory.

Burst of brilliance
You come
As death proceeds.

Oh, little leaf of green,
Your color changes
And gushes forth as gold,

Only as you die.

Colors hidden formerly
Erupt boldly on the scene
As the leaves prepare to drop.

Burst of brilliance at death;
As it is with leaves,
So it is with me.

Burst of brilliance comes
When I recede,
And Jesus advances.

Burst of brilliance comes
When I die to self;
And Jesus lives in me.

And for all the burst of brilliance known on earth,
None will e're compare
To the radiance we'll see

When death takes us finally.

Color there – indescribable.
Creation there – perfected.
People there – as they ought to be.

God, remind me that both now and then –
The burst of brilliance comes
At the death of me.

Sweet Waters, Sweet Life

When they came to Marah, they could not drink the waters of Marah,
for they were bitter; therefore it was named Marah. So the people grumbled at
Moses, saying, "What shall we drink?" Then he cried out to the LORD, and the
LORD showed him a tree; and he threw it into the waters,
and the waters became sweet.

Exodus 15:22-25a

Following the miraculous parting of the Red Sea, God's people travelled into the wilderness. After three long days, they had still found no water. The only refreshment discovered had been the waters of Marah, which were bitter — too bitter to drink. As thirsty people would, the Israelites complained and asked their leader, Moses, how their thirst might now possibly be quenched. Moses knew exactly what to do; he cried out to God. After all, the Savior who divided the sea that his people might cross on dry ground could surely now lead them to water.

And God did provide. However, the Lord did not take them to a new place for sustenance. Rather, he transformed the old place. God showed Moses a tree. Moses threw that tree into the bitter waters of Marah. Suddenly, the formerly unpalatable water became sweet. Thirst was quenched, and life could be lived.

The peculiar fashion in which our timeless God worked for His thirsty people thousands of years ago indicates the way in which He now works for us. When we find life bitter and intolerable, God points to a tree to make life sweet and livable.

Who of us can swallow the distress of a guilty conscience? Who of us can live vigorously while dying of thirst for peace with a holy God? Who of us can tolerate the difficulty and disaster of life without assurance that we will someday know joy unhindered? Who of us can find the sweetness of life while the bitterness of guilt gnaws at our core? None can. Not one.

God points to the tree, the tree of Calvary. He bids us throw that tree into the mess and anguish of our sin. When that tree touches my soul, the dilemma is solved because the anguish of my sin is placed square on Jesus Christ.

Hebrews 9:14 proclaims, "How much more will the blood of Christ, who through the eternal Spirit offered Himself without blemish to God, cleanse your conscience from dead works to serve the living God?" The blood of Jesus shed on the tree of Calvary is placed into my life to make all things well. With a clean conscience is the only way to live a sweet life.

Our lives can be transformed so that we may live in peace, just as the water of Marah could be made right to drink. God transformed the water by throwing a tree into the mix. He transforms our lives by presenting the tree of Calvary to the horror of our sin, thereby neutralizing sin's effect with the sacrifice of His Son. What formerly seemed intolerable – our guilt-ridden life – is now a true delight.

Nothin' Wrong with Weary

So Jesus, wearied as He was from His journey, was sitting beside the well.
John 4:6 (ESV)

Even though I feel bone-tired, can God still use me? Is my exhaustion a sign that He is not pleased with me?

Remember the woman at the well – the Samaritan who needed the burden of her sinful past lifted? How did that miraculous, life-changing encounter begin? "So Jesus, *wearied as He was from His journey*, was sitting beside the well" (John 4:6, ESV, emphasis mine). What? Did I read that correctly? Yes! It was the weariness of Jesus that led Him to sit and rest by the well. It was, in fact, the toiling effects of Jesus' journey that sparked this eternal event!

Just to be sure that Jesus felt what I feel, I checked out the Greek words behind John's writing. This account means that Jesus grew weary, felt tired, and toiled; He knew the repercussion of bodily labor. Ah, Jesus, thank You that You know how I feel. Thank You for showing me that from my life can stream eternal workings even though I have paused in the midst of exhaustion.

I will now trust for the miraculous inner workings of God's own Spirit to happen through my life, my body, my words, and my hands . . . even though my human frailty is right there with me.

Not a Hoof Left Behind

Therefore, our livestock too shall go with us; not a hoof shall be left behind, for we shall take some of them to serve the LORD our God. And until we arrive there, we ourselves do not know with what we shall serve the LORD.

Exodus 10:26

There exists nothing that is off limits to God. I do not mean just the general stuff of the universe; I mean the very things of our own lives. Everything – absolutely everything – must be yielded to the Lord if we hope to walk in His freedom.

Who knows what God will require of us? The one thing that is certain is that He expects our willingness to give to Him anything. Therefore, at all times we must stand ready to hand over some particular component of our lives.

When exasperated by the plague of darkness over the land of Egypt, Pharaoh angrily told Moses to leave Egypt with all the people, including the Israelite children. However, Pharaoh stipulated that the Israelite flocks and herds be left behind. One can only imagine how tempting it might have been for Moses to take the offer and run, given the horror suffered by the enslaved Hebrew nation to that point. But Moses remembered God's clear directive to leave the Egyptian land in order to worship the Lord. An exit at this point would be disobedient; a departure under these circumstances would prohibit Moses and the Hebrews from offering whatever sacrifice God would require.

Moses stands wholeheartedly before the God He trusts and proclaims to the powerful Egyptian ruler that he and his people will not leave without every last Israelite animal. Moses explains that God will require some of those animals as sacrifices; and because it is not currently known which ones, all must go with them.

How accurate a portrayal of the stance each Christian must have when it comes to the proper entrance to freedom! We do not yet know what God will require of us, so we will take everything with us to Him in anticipation of our sacrifice!

The final plague – the death of the firstborn – will bring the ultimate deliverance of the Israelite people. Ironically, that plague is brought on by Moses' refusal to leave Egypt without every last animal. Had Moses given in and left without all of God's require- ments, what would have happened? In God's scheme of things, the willingness to give it all precipitates the genuine freedom we gain because of the death – and resurrection – of Jesus.

Do not hold back. Know that God requires everything. Do not allow the difficulty of yielding any and all of your life to stop the Lord's plan of deliverance for you. Let the words of trusting Moses resonate in your mind, "Not a hoof shall be left behind."

When UNDERNEATH Is More Important than OVERCOME

Though the LORD is on high, he looks upon the lowly, but the proud
he knows from afar.

Psalm 138:6 (NIV)

Have you ever failed? You prayed, you hoped, you tried . . . and you failed. You really meant to overcome. But there you were, unable to succeed.

I recently had another opportunity to prevail in a particular area of trusting the Lord in which I had failed numerous times before. Were I to share the circumstance, some might say it is no big deal. Yet, it is a big deal, because I have tried again and again to commit this fear to the Lord and be one who overcomes.

I returned home having to hang my head as I realized how weak I truly am. I cannot even wholly trust the Lord in an area so many others find so simple. As I began mentally to beat up myself, our God of everlasting mercy spoke gently to my heart.

"It is more important to humbly realize your dependence on Me than to be proud of your own self," He seemed to say. "In my infinite wisdom there are times when I know it is more important to be *underneath* my mercy than to *overcome* the circumstance," I felt Him whisper.

Oh, Lord, this is difficult for an aspiring perfectionist such as me. Yet, I feel so safe knowing God is working on the core of who I am.

This musing of mine is not an excuse for failure or lack of trust in anybody's life. Rather, it is a call to remember who's who! God is God, and I depend wholly on Him. My only strength comes in knowing – and having to be reminded – that I am a humble human being who desperately needs Jesus to hold me every step of the way. My striving and subsequent failure vividly brings this dependence to the forefront.

King David knew the secret; He had been brought low by many encounters with his own sin and inadequacies. Thus, he said, "Though the Lord is on high, He looks upon the lowly, but the proud He knows from afar."

When we are lowly, brought down by circumstances and our own finite humanity; let it remind us of the beauty of humility in God's sight. Let it focus our minds on a God whose love and mercy are so pervasive that He chooses to strive with lowly people like us.

I love you, Lord, for reaching *down* to me.

Take the Long View

The Rock! His work is perfect, For all His ways are just; a God of faithfulness and without injustice, Righteous and upright is He.

Deuteronomy 32:4

What bold words Moses speaks forth in his declaration of the supreme goodness of God. The leader of renown assesses God after many years of living and serving, and Moses concludes that God's work is perfect. As we ponder the leader's reflection, let me remind you of a few elements of Moses' life: He was hidden in a basket on the Nile River because of Pharaoh's edict that he and other Hebrew boys be murdered, he was raised in a foreign home, he bore the realization that he was separated from his people, he risked his life and comfort to identify with the people of God, he grappled with his murder of an Egyptian, he lived in obscurity for forty years in Midian, he was asked to help deliver the Israelites despite personal weaknesses, he endured the increased misery of the Israelites when he first approached Pharaoh with God's commands, he believed God through the plagues and death of the first-born, he faced the dilemma of standing between the Red Sea and the approaching Egyptians, he led a complaining people through the wilderness forty years, and – most of all – he sustained personal devastation when denied entry to the Promised Land because of his own disobedience when he struck a rock instead of speaking to it as God commanded.

The bottom line is that Moses withstood grave disappointment at many instances of his life, and he suffered under baffling circumstances at many points. Were the "snapshot" view of things the final answer, Moses may not have declared his unwavering confidence in God's inability to ever do wrong.

Despite the seemingly intolerable hardship at many turns along the road of life, Moses proclaimed, "His work is perfect." Perfect here in the Hebrew means "complete, whole, healthful, having

24

integrity." Moses learned a vital key with God: take the long view. We may not apprehend the purpose of any particular difficulty or heartbreak, but we realize that God completes the picture of every righteous person's life. He commands that all of life – even the grueling parts – function to fulfill a work in us that results in what is best, what is sound, what is fit.

Speaking of a long view, I stand amazed that Moses declares the complete justice of God even though he knew that he had been denied entrance to the Promised Land. Deuteronomy 3:23-27 makes clear that Moses sought God's restoration and begged for entrance to Canaan. God denied him. And yet – with valor that inspires – Moses pronounces the faithfulness of God and the perfection of His work.

How does Moses' broken heart exude such a hope? He has worked for God all his days and now is stopped at the threshold of a life dream. Or was he? All of Moses' contemporaries who crossed over into the Promised Land died. Despite their entrance to Canaan; they faced enemies, difficulties, illnesses, and every other plight of humanity. The earthly Promised Land is not *the* Promised Land; it is not the ultimate dream.

Hebrews 11:13-16 says that great men and women of God have died *in faith*, without receiving the promises. They welcomed the promises from a distance. They believed and confessed that their true home is a heavenly home. Moses is in this category of unbelievable believers who stood on hills overlooking the earthly Promised Land and knew for a fact that they *would* enter the Promised Land – the heavenly one!

Some will accuse people like me of using Heaven as a crutch. They might say that Heaven is not an answer to the turmoil we face in this world. I believe God has an infinite future to correct all wrongs and fill all dreams to an infinite depth. In Hebrews 11:16, we are informed that God is not ashamed to be called our God *when and if* we desire a heavenly city. For God, the heavenly Promised

Land is not "pie in the sky" stuff. To the Maker of all reality, Heaven is the most real and the most desired. He prides Himself in those of us who, like Moses, truly believe that our deepest answers await us.

Let us announce, as Moses did, that God's work is perfect. Despite anything we face, He does no wrong. Moreover, He has prepared a city for us!

What's this World Coming To?

When he has done this, then the Son himself will be made subject to him who put everything under him, so that God may be all in all.

I Corinthians 15:28 (NIV)

"What is this world coming to?" someone might ask in disgust. When we see evidence of the culture's rebellion against God, when we become frustrated with the circumstances of our own lives, and when we are shocked by bad news; we may ask that infamous question ourselves, "What is this world coming to?"

The world is coming to something. Here it is: **God will be all in all**! He will have the final word, fulfill the final plan, and give to us who love and serve Him all for which our hearts could possibly long.

One of my favorite chapters in the Word of God is I Corinthians 15. Written by the Holy Spirit through the Apostle Paul, the chapter emphasizes the resurrection of the dead. Not only does Paul discuss the resurrection of Jesus from the dead, but he assures us that we, too, will rise from the dead because of Jesus!

In I Corinthians 15, God explains that Jesus will conquer every enemy at the close of earthly history. In other words, He will blow away all the nasty plans of the devil and all the ways Satan has tried to destroy us and our faith in God. He will forever rid the universe of heartache, disease, and natural devastation. The last enemy Jesus will obliterate for us is death. After Jesus conquers death, He will undoubtedly hand everything over to God the Father so that God may be all in all (verse 28).

Here is a thoughtful and crucial question: if the final goal is that God be all in all, what should be the goal of every moment? If God Almighty is pushing all circumstances toward His ultimate will, why are we not doing our best to do the same? The end of the world as we know it is not confusion and chaos; it is the culmination of all things for the glory of God Himself. This will happen no matter how much resistance humans put forth. But, we – as God's people – should not only avoid resistance against God's plan, we should actively work toward God's goal.

If we could just whittle down every tiny moment to its real purpose – to glorify God – what would happen? How great would we feel as we fall in line with the conclusive, grand plan of God? If I could think as I walk down the hall, "What kind of smile would glorify God?" or as I work at my job, "What kind of effort would glorify God?" or as I choose my entertainment, "What kind of movie would glorify God?" or as I interact with my colleagues, "What kind of behavior would glorify God?" or as I talk on my cell phone, "What kind of conversation would glorify God?" then what kind of life would I be living? **One that aligns with the ultimate reality of what the world is coming to**!

Why the Wilderness When I Want Happiness?

God did not lead them by the way of the land of the Philistines, even though it was near; for God said, "The people might change their minds when they see war, and return to Egypt." Hence God led the people around by the way of the wilderness to the Red Sea . . .

Exodus 13:17b-18a

Avoidance of pain is currently upheld as one of the greatest of aspirations. "What can God do for me that will make my life better, easier, and more palatable?" we ask. Isn't a happy life a natural outcome of salvation?

Perhaps we need to go back to square one and be reminded of salvation's essence. In Biblical terms, to be saved means to be delivered from sin's power and consequence. First and foremost, we are sinful people who need drastic deliverance from our bent toward evil. The problem is not our material discomfort or our lack of satisfaction; the problem is that our very nature – and our actions – offend a holy God. God's sacrifice of His own Son for our sinfulness brings our deliverance. A person who trusts in the atonement of Jesus is covered with His righteousness. That is deliverance. It is a pronouncement of being right – despite who we are – because we trust in Jesus.

Now, let us go back to the original question, "Isn't a happy life a natural outcome of salvation?" Maybe we should be asking a different question, "Isn't our salvation – our deliverance – the *most* important thing?" What could be more important than my hell-bent soul finding deliverance from sin? What is more vital than they eyes of my heart being fixed intensely on the God who saves me? What is more critical than my direct journey to the home of ultimate righteousness God is preparing for me?

In God's estimation, there is nothing – simply *nothing* – more important than our deliverance. In fact, when God miraculously delivered the Israelites from slavery to Egypt, He chose to send them the long way to the Promised Land – through the wilderness. Why such a difficult path to traverse? Exodus 13:17b-18a makes clear, "God did not lead them by the way of the land of the Philistines, even though it was near; for God said, 'The people might change their minds when they see war, and return to Egypt.' Hence God led the people around by the way of the wilderness to the Red Sea."

The wilderness would be difficult, with challenges galore. However, the short route through Philistia meant a direct turning back. God knew His people would be too quickly tempted to go back to bondage in Egypt, and they would then never reach the Promised Land.

So it is. The wilderness of our lives can be sadly difficult. Truly, only God Himself knows why we must travel the path we do. But, one thing we know for a fact: *the avoidance of pain is simply not more important than our full deliverance*. I will travel this wilderness path, since I know it means I will not turn back. I will see God one day in the place He resides.

How Much Is Enough?

Keep your life free from the love of money, and be content with what you have, for he has said, "I will never leave you nor forsake you."
Hebrews 13:5-6 (ESV)

In a culture of greed and reckless spending, each one of us must ask, "How much is enough?" A resounding answer comes directly from God's own Word, "Whatever you have right now is enough."

That's right. Whatever we have at the moment shall be enough for us. Our hearts shall be at rest in this instant. Another car, a larger home, a stylish new outfit, one more of the latest electronic gadgets, a larger television screen, more expensive furniture — none of these things should increase our fulfillment one bit. The blessings in our possession at this moment should be enough to keep us content.

Why? How can we actually be satisfied, before we obtain something just a little better than what we have right now? This is how. This is why. God is with us and He will not walk away.

One way to know if I am in obedience to the first and greatest commandment as stated by Jesus in Matthew 22:37-38, is to ask myself if I am contented right now. Is there a joy in my heart and deepest satisfaction in my soul even though I do not currently possess things I might like to possess? Or is my mind often drifting to thoughts of what I could have? My mind should be focused on my Savior because He fills my heart so fully that joy overflows no matter the status of my list of material possessions.

God has commanded us to keep our character free from the love of money. He goes on to demand that we be content with what we have. But God does not ask this difficult thing of His people without informing us of the way to accomplish it. He says we ought to be satisfied with what we have because He will never leave us or forsake us.

As one great hymn proclaims, God is the fountain of all blessing. If I have God, I have everything that is possible for a human being to have. The One who made everything and owns everything is my Lord. He alone brings the joy that properly accompanies any blessing He gives. Even the wing of a butterfly or the petal of a flower or a beam of the sunlight can stir my heart with unspeakable joy and mystery. Just the bite of an apple or a gulp of cold water brings amazing satisfaction. The smile of a child or the hug of a friend is an experience never to be traded. I find I do not need more; I need Jesus to make what I have more than I could ever imagine.

Since God promises to never abandon me, I know He will provide for me what is necessary in the next moment, next day, next year, or next decade. He is the Source of all existence, and He is the One responsible for His own children. If I am solely responsible to provide for myself, I know my devices and best efforts can fail; and – even if they don't – someday I will finally fail when this body gives out in death. But, if I trust my God, He can bring to pass anything in any instant while I traverse this world. And, when I go to the next world, my eternal God will provide everything there!

We need not be worried about what we do not have. In fact, we are commanded by God to protect our hearts from the love of money and discontentment. We are admonished, rather, to focus on God's presence with us. Let us make a commitment to refuse to sin against our God with a discontented, greedy heart. Let us make a commitment to focus on Him and His faithfulness. For, He is the Provider.

Twice the Courage

I have told you these things, so that in me you may have peace. In this world you will have trouble. But take heart! I have overcome the world.

John 16:33 (NIV)

We ought to thank Jesus continually for His honesty. The Biblical Christian worldview is the accurate view, because it accounts for all aspects of life – including the trouble. As our Lord was getting ready to go to the cross and preparing His disciples for the coming of the Holy Spirit, Jesus reminded His followers that life would be rough. He said, "In this world you will have trouble." How true! When we repeat this statement of Jesus, we may do so with a tone of affirmation, or meekly through a veil of tears. Why? Because one thing we know is that trouble is part of our lives.

The Greek word for trouble here is one that means "a pressing" or "pressure." The difficulties and heartbreaks of life press in on us, and Satan's hope is that we would cave in under the strain. After all, his goal is to destroy us (John 10:10). When the crushing force of tribulation comes, do not give in through thoughts of hopelessness! Refuse to allow your vision to be limited to what is temporal! Trust in the God is who is bigger than the burden!

The answer Jesus gave to the tribulation of His people is not that the trials would disappear. No, Jesus loves us enough to tell us the truth. Things will get wild, my friends. You will suffer and be persecuted. You will face hardships sometimes unimaginable, sometimes just enough to deter your focus.

Here is the answer Jesus gives, "Take heart! I have overcome the world." The original language behind "take heart" is "be of good courage." In fact, Jesus uses the verb two times in a row here. He actually says, "Be of good courage; be of good courage." Okay. I need the second reminder. Jesus drives the point home. He does not simply give mediocre courage; my courage in Him is doubly sure!

Our Savior also says, "In me you may have peace." The Greek gets to the heart of the requirement, as it informs us that we are to "have, possess, or lay hold of" the peace. The unredeemed person may believe that peace is some wishy-washy concept, or that peace is impersonal and just floats down upon people who desire it. Quite to the contrary, peace is strong and personal. Peace can only be found in the Savior, and it is something of which we must really lay hold. We must walk with Jesus and determine to be blessed by His strength in the midst of difficulty.

The kind of peace Jesus offers is real. It is not the blind faith of those who do not know Him and are just "hoping for the best." Jesus boldly proclaims in this verse, "I have overcome the world." Indeed, He has! The world can certainly "bring it on" as far as crushing heartache and troubling circumstances, but Jesus has overcome the world. He stands transcendent over everything that happens. He is weaving together the circumstances of the entire universe to fulfill His plan. The word for "world" here is the same word from which we get "cosmos." God is telling us that He has overcome the aggregate of all things earthly; all the world affairs – personally and nationally – are under His sovereignty. There is no doubt that I will witness His grand deliverance and resolution with my own eyes. This reminds me of the words of the great man, Job, who declared, "I know that my Redeemer lives, and that in the end he will stand upon the earth. And after my skin has been destroyed, yet in my flesh I will see God" (Job 19:25-26, NIV).

As the pressure comes, trust in the Overcomer of the Cosmos. The courage He gives is doubly strong.

Jesus Can't Be Your Example
Until He's Your Savior

Here is a trustworthy saying that deserves full acceptance: Christ Jesus came into the world to save sinners – of whom I am the worst.

I Timothy 1:15 (NIV)

Recently I perused some children's books that had been labeled as "Christian." While reviewing these works, I was reminded of how subtly the truth can be undermined. One of the children's books was a survey of major stories of the Bible. Each two-page summary of a Biblical event was accompanied by colorful drawings and a quick prayer to summarize the heart of the message. Most unfortunately, the author missed the main point of many of the Biblical accounts.

As I read through the pages dealing with the crucifixion and resurrection of Jesus, I was gravely disappointed to realize that the book did not refer to Jesus' work as our Savior. It recommended that children look to Jesus as an example about how to forgive others and how to reach out to others, but it did not mention the fact that Jesus died on the Cross for our sins. In fact – to the best of my examination – the book never mentioned the word "sin."

How tragic. What would be even more catastrophic is if adults reading the book did not realize that sin was not mentioned. This inconspicuous removal of anything related to the sinful nature of humans and our need for redemption is eternally harmful.

The message the powers of darkness would like us to believe is that we can simply follow the example of Christ and other "holy" people. The lie is that Jesus is only the role model that all of us should employ when making decisions. To naturalists, He is mistakenly a fully self-actualized human; to new age believers, He is wrongly assumed to be a person genuinely in touch with His divinity and having reached the higher plane; but – in truth – He is God come to earth in flesh to save humans from sin.

Weary people – who are bound by sin, and burdened by the wrong thoughts and behaviors that we cannot escape on our own – need a Savior! We do not require a fine example – or even a perfect example – of *how* to live; we need a God who can *enable* us to live. Once the Savior delivers us from our sin nature, then – and only then – can we begin to live rightly.

The apostle Paul said it wonderfully in I Timothy 1:15 (NIV), "Here is a trustworthy saying that deserves full acceptance: Christ Jesus came into the world to save sinners – of whom I am the worst." This, my friends, is why Jesus came. He came to endure the wrath of God for our sins that we might be free from the sin curse.

It may not be fashionable in today's culture to seemingly downgrade the human condition this way, but it is certainly the truth. And every person who feels the weight of sin knows another example of goodness is not what they need. Jesus simply cannot be my example until He is my Savior! To be bound by sin is to be spiritually dead. Dead people cannot follow examples. Dead people need life. God – through Jesus – gives dead people life. After He does, then these people can do right.

The crux of the matter is spelled out simply in Ephesians 2:4-5 (NIV), "But because of his great love for us, God, who is rich in mercy, made us alive with Christ even when we were dead in transgressions – it is by grace you have been saved."

My prayer is that weary sinners find new life in Jesus as the Savior. I also pray that God will cause us to see where truth is lacking, or only half-proclaimed. People's lives depend on it. God, please help us.

Tracing God's Heart on the
Mount of Olives

In that day His feet will stand on the Mount of Olives, which is in front of
Jerusalem on the east; and the Mount of Olives will be split in its middle from
east to west by a very large valley, so that half of the mountain will move
toward the north and the other half toward the south.

Zechariah 14:4

Today in the Middle East, just to the right of Jerusalem, stands the Mount of Olives. This mountain is separated from the great city by a narrow area called the Kidron Valley. The Mount of Olives is approximately one mile long and rises to 2,680 feet above sea level. This mountain tells us much about the heart of God; for, God is the God of geography and history. Too many people today think the true God is "spiritual only," but He is God over every realm! He is Lord over geography because He made this terrestrial ball and the entire universe (Psalm 121:2), and He is Lord over history because He stands outside of time as the "Beginning and the End" (Revelation 22:13).

What does this actual, geographical location reveal to us about the heart of God? Let's look at three things:

1) In Luke 21:37, we learn that Jesus would actually rest on the Mount of Olives following long days of teaching disciples. Our Savior would close His eyes and sleep on the mount at night. This amazes me, because Matthew 26:38 reveals that at this same place – the Mount of Olives – Jesus was nearly over-whelmed by the weight of the sacrifice He would make for the sins of the world. You see, the Garden of Gethsemane – where Jesus prayed right before His arrest and crucifixion – lies on the western slope of the Mount of Olives. Our Savior commenced His unimaginable suffering at the very place He rested so many other days before. I am ashamed to say that there have been times I can hardly sleep at night if I know I have an impending

difficult time ahead; yet, Jesus rested in the very place where He knew He would carry the weight of human sin. Jesus Christ could rest because He knew that His plan would prevail in the end, no matter how dark the time at hand.

The Mount of Olives reminds us that we can rest in the midst of difficult circumstances and while facing an unknown future because God is in control.

2) The words of Acts 1:9-12 tell us that Jesus Christ left this earth from the Mount of Olives. After instructing the disciples that they should concentrate on spending their lives as a testimony to God by the power of the Holy Spirit dwelling in them, Jesus was taken up into a cloud and was drawn out of sight. The disciples no doubt stood dumbfounded. They had finally wrapped their minds around His divinity because He had risen from the dead just as the Scripture promised, and He had walked on the earth for forty days following His resurrection. Now, after those seemingly short forty days, He was leaving! Their mouths probably hung open as they watched Him go. Perhaps they were thinking, "Why is He leaving us after rising from the dead?" and "Why is He not fixing this world system right now; why is He allowing the Romans to continue in their plot?" and "When will we see Him again?" As those disciples stood there, two angels informed them that "this Jesus" will come back the same way He left.

I love it! "This Jesus"! Not another Jesus, but the very same One who walked with them, hugged them, ate with them, was nailed to a cross for them, resurrected for them, walked with them again in His *new, glorified* body; and ate fish with them in His new, glorified body – *this* Jesus would return to *this* earth! The Jesus that was put in the tomb is the Jesus that came out of the tomb and is the Jesus who will return one day. Similarly, the same me that dies physically is the same me that will rise physically and enjoy what Jesus prepares one day. Because of Him, we live too!

The Mount of Olives reminds us that a very real Jesus is coming back to this earth to make a home of righteousness for us to enjoy with Him in very real, glorified bodies.

3) The prophet Zechariah declares in Zechariah 14:4 that one future day the feet of Jesus will stand again on the Mount of Olives. At some point before the second coming of Christ, great armies will go to battle against Jerusalem. The city will be captured, and the end of Jerusalem and its inhabitants will seem inevitable. But, just when things seem hopeless – and not before – Jesus will descend on that mount. His feet will cause the Mount of Olives to split in half, producing a valley between the newly formed northern and southern halves of the mountain. That valley will be the way of escape for the inhabitants of Jerusalem. Zechariah goes on to explain that the inauguration of the millennial reign of Christ will mean the people of Jerusalem will dwell securely, with no more curse (Zechariah 14:11).

Just as God provided a way of escape for His people when they were caught between the Red Sea and the approaching Egyptians, so He will provide a way of escape when the Antichrist and all the godless armies seek to destroy God's remnant of people. Nothing stops God's plan. In a real and tangible way, Jesus will once again be seen on the Mount of Olives.

The Mount of Olives reminds us that Jesus is in charge of this world and all of history. He will provide the way of escape for His people and usher in the beginning of His perfect kingdom.

Allow the God of all history and geography to strengthen your heart with the truths about one, particular location in the Middle East. The Mount of Olives is very important to Jesus, and it should be very important to us, too.

This Is (Not?) Too Much for Me

No temptation has overtaken you but such as is common to man; and God is faithful, who will not allow you to be tempted beyond what you are able, but with the temptation will provide the way of escape also, so that you will be able to endure it.

I Corinthians 10:13

I know the tribulation of life can feel this way, but – for the Christian – it cannot accurately be said that a trial is simply "too much for me." Oh, I have surely felt at my literal wit's end in deep places of despair and struggle, but the Word of God stands true forever. Paul said triumphantly in I Corinthians 10:13, "No temptation has overtaken you but such as is common to man; and God is faithful, who will not allow you to be tempted beyond what you are able, but with the temptation will provide the way of escape also, so that you will be able to endure it."

Either we believe in the God of the Bible or we do not. As a Christian who trusts God for my salvation, I must certainly also trust Him for my survival through difficulty. How can I claim the miracle that He saves me from the wrath my sin deserves, but I cannot also believe the miracle that He provides my way to escape the temptation to sin or to give up?

I Corinthians 10:13 outlines five important facts remember:

1) **Every trial we undergo is common to the human race.** Despite our tendency to think we are the only ones who have ever felt the way we do, God ensures that our trials are not out of the realm of human experience or toleration.
2) **God is faithful even though we are not.** Too often we view God the way we view ourselves or other people. We tend to think that God will act with us the way we might act with others. We imagine that He could possibly give up on His own people. Yet, God is transcendent – completely different

40

than us. He has promised to remain faithful to those who desire Him. He promises that – despite our unfaithfulness – He will never let us down in the midst of greatest difficulty. No matter the trial, He will stay with us to provide a way to obedience and victory.

3) **God will not give to us more than we can endure.** The God who created our physical bodies and our emotional, mental and spiritual make-up certainly ascertains and measures precisely the trials we go through. He knows far better than we do just exactly what we can handle.

4) **God always provides a way of escape.** In other words, God will surely give to us what we need to flee the temptation to disobey and cave to Satan's tactics. God does this by making clear to us a route of escape. Remember the Israelites stuck between the approaching Egyptian chariots and the waters of the Red Sea? God made a route of escape through the sea. God did it. The Israelites simply followed the way God provided. So it is in our current trial. God provides the way for us to make it through, though our minds may see only trouble behind and before.

5) **God's plan is that we endure, not be destroyed.** I know it feels as though this will be the end of you, but that is not God's plan. He provides a way of escape that you may be able to endure. He wants you to press forward in your walk with Him, and finally – one blessed day – make it to your heavenly home.

Yes, our hearts break under the weight of anguish and difficulties of many kinds. However, let's take God at His Word. Let's memorize and ponder and live out the truth of I Corinthians 10:13. Then we can say, "This is *not* too much for me, for my God is faithful."

Does Everything End with Us?

Then God said, "Let us make man in Our image, according to Our likeness. . . "
Genesis 1:26

Genuine Christianity results in a radically countercultural worldview. There is no way around this fact. The heart of Biblical Christianity is "God first." The heart of today's culture is "me first." One need not be a philosophy scholar to recognize the law of non-contradiction at play here. Either it is God first or me first, but it cannot be both at the same time.

I recently fell into the cultural trap when I found myself praying that God would reveal to me what His plan for my life was in reference to certain circumstances swirling about me. I basically kept begging God to show me what He has for me. Feeling stressed and at times sorry for myself, I wanted to know how God would help me. This seems innocent at the surface, but the truth hit me like a brick after many months of praying in this general way and not receiving peace. The Lord then showed me, "Shelli, it's not about what I have for you, but what you have for Me," He seemed to say. I realized that God was impressing on me this thought, "My life is to be spent for His sake – no matter the cost. The answer is not in finding how God fits into my plan and my life, but how I fit into God's plan!"

Stepping back from my own encounter with the false worldview of self-centeredness, I began to ponder what has happened in recent times. Most of the marketing to which we are constantly exposed urges us to buy what will help us feel better about ourselves and give us a sense of fulfillment of our self-determined needs. We are prodded to buy gadgets that can be customized to our lifestyle and our personality, and that can satisfy our every whim. As Christians, we need to discern the empty philosophy behind this strategy, and boldly determine to think as God will have us think – even if that means dismantling in our own lives the pull of the marketplace. I know it can be difficult to imagine the general marketplace could be wrong, but remember that we do not use the world as our compass. God's unchanging Word is our standard.

What is the source of the "me first" culture in which we find ourselves? I believe it can be traced back to a pantheistic view that followed the period of modernism. A New Age type of thinking recently invaded our culture. The crux of this pantheism is explained well by Dean Halverson (2003),

> As the existence of a transcendent God who created all things is denied, which is what the New Age movement does, then the objectivity – the solidness, the otherness – of external reality is diminished. When that happens, then the role of the individual in shaping reality increases in importance. (177)

Pantheism is a belief that everything is god. Divinity is one, and people are an emanation of that "oneness." Pantheism dangerously says that God is not "other than us" or "outside of us," but that He is the same as us. Since we are divine (of course, it takes much contemplative meditation and striving to realize this), we have much to do with reality. In fact, Pantheists believe that we – in essence – create our own reality.

A pantheistic framework flowed easily into the idea of hyperindividualism that is so prevalent today. Matthew Vos (2010/2011) explains,

> Another social change influencing schools and students hails from the hyperindividualism saturating the Western world. Television advertisements promote products that can be created, customized, and ordered to reflect the "real you." Cars, iPods, computers, and pizzas can all be fashioned to your image and to your liking. (22)

The culture's worldview shifted easily from a general paradigm of pantheism to the specific problem of hyperindividualism. We humans have a much too inflated sense of ourselves and our role in reality when compared to God and His role in reality.

People in general have largely come to believe that the stuff of life is supposed to reflect us and be what we want it to be. We have come to feel that everything ends with us. Actually, we are not the end of the line. We are designed to point to God; the purpose of our lives is to glorify Him. Though we are yet sinners, we were created in His image (Genesis 1:26). The point of living is to make God the most important thing. It follows that the stuff of life is to reflect Him, too. Romans 1:20 declares that the entire creation tells us things about God.

Do we see the difference in thinking presented to us? It is not that the stuff of life points to us, but that we point to God. In turn, we harness this creation and use all He has given to bring glory to Him.

I realize now that the purpose of my life is to be used by God for His renown. My purpose is not to conform my experiences and circumstances to fit what I deem as a good or comfortable life (hyperindividualism streaming from pantheistic thought). The culture can present to me whatever slick marketing messages it wants, but I know that the Maker of Reality is my Maker. I am not an emanation from God; I am a creation of God. My life will be spent bringing glory to Him for as long as He gives me strength to do so in this world, and then He will supply the strength for me to do so forever in the world to come. May we quit trying to manipulate circumstances to "create the reality" we desire, and – instead – gratefully endure all things as God is exalted.

Magnanimous Mercy

Then all the disciples left Him and fled.

Matthew 26:56b

One of the saddest sentences in the Bible is this one: "Then all the disciples left Him and fled" (Matthew 26:56b). Wow. Just as Jesus was being arrested in the Garden of Gethsemane, His closest friends and followers abandoned Him.

Jesus had faithfully kept His word for three earthly years, serving alongside His disciples. Now at this time of deepest despair – right when Jesus was about to begin this period of unimaginable suffering – His followers walk away. Shame on them! Should not they have realized what was happening? Should not they have understood that Jesus had predicted this event and its outcome? Should not they have stood by Him because of their love for Him? Should not their own fear and selfishness have been set aside for the sake of the Savior?

No, I cannot say, "Shame on them." For each one of them is me. I walk away at times. I am faithless more often than I like to count. I abandon my Lord at various times of difficulty. I forget His promises. I am much like each disciple: I often fail my Jesus, though I hate the thought.

Thank God that "He Himself knows our frame; He is mindful that we are but dust" (Psalm 103:14). For, though the disciples fled right before His crucifixion, Jesus still died for them. Jesus did not choose to go back on His promise of redemption even though His closest friends abandoned Him right as He was about to embark on the darkest moments of His earthly life. We can barely understand that kind of love. However, finite understanding does not negate this love's reality.

Forty days after His Resurrection, Jesus looked at the same disciples who had forsaken Him and boldly proclaimed, "You will receive power when the Holy Spirit has come upon you; and you shall be my witnesses both in Jerusalem, and in all Judea and Samaria, and even to the remotest part of the earth" (Acts 1:8). A second "wow" is fitting here. The ones who had been faithless were now entrusted with the greatest task imaginable: being a witness to the world by the power of the living God inside of them.

God, may we, too – though we have failed you at times – be entrusted with Your calling. May we grasp the depths of your magnanimous mercy. Those disciples went out more invigorated than ever because they experienced the profound forgiveness of Jesus. The ones who had fled the scene in fear now gave their own lives away for Jesus' sake.

His mercy changes things – for the better.

God Is Bigger than the Plan

Many are the plans in a man's heart, but it is the LORD's purpose that prevails.
Proverbs 19:21 (NIV)

Lately I have been pondering plans. You know – plans of all kinds – long term, short term, strategic, five-year, selfish, unselfish, corporate level, personal, realistic and unrealistic.

We live in a world of plans and schemes and hopes and dreams. Encouraged at every turn to map out our lives and careers, we devise many scenarios. We feel pressured to articulate the steps of next week, next month, next year, and so on and on and on.

Orderliness is of God. The mathematician in me cries out on behalf of logic and regularity. As human beings created in the image of God, we ought to strive for order and design. However, we need to remember that we are just that – *created in the image of God*. God alone stands transcendent, above and outside His creation. He is, therefore, unable to fail, never confused, unaffected by wrong passion, clearly able to see the future, powerful enough to clear obstacles, wise enough to differentiate between obstacles and blessings, and loving enough to desire our best even when we cannot understand His working.

Proverbs 19:21 (NIV) declares, "Many are the plans in a man's heart, but it is the LORD's purpose that prevails." Our plans originate in our hearts. God's purpose originates with God. I am the created. He is the Creator. I have many plans. He has one purpose. The only way my plans make any sense is as I seek to align them with His will. And even then, in my limited understanding, I can misinterpret the will of God. I can selfishly confuse what I want with what God wants. Let us therefore be sure to put God before the plan. To us, the plan seems so big. But the plan is so much smaller than God.

Having recently earned a graduate degree in educational leadership, I know the value of strategic plans. Having been created by a transcendent God, I know He is bigger. If my plans come to pass because God sees fit to bring them about, so be it. If God's purpose supersedes what I had in mind, so be it as well. If I exalt my ideas above His, I am hopeless. If I exalt Him above my ideas, I may just see my ideas coordinate with His purpose!

The Essence of Noah's Salvation

The LORD smelled the pleasing aroma and said in his heart: "Never again will I curse the ground because of man, even though every inclination of his heart is evil from childhood.

Genesis 10:21a (NIV)

Here is a question: "Why did God destroy the earth by flood in Noah's day?" Answer: "Mankind was very, very bad." Here is a second question: "Why did God spare Noah and his family?" Typical answer: "Noah was a good man who obeyed God." Let us get to the heart of both questions and both answers.

First, it is true that God destroyed the world by flood in Noah's day because of evil. Genesis 6:5-8 (NIV) says, "The LORD saw how great man's wickedness on the earth had become, and that every inclination of the thoughts of his heart was only evil all the time. The Lord was grieved that He had made man on earth, and His heart was filled with pain. So the Lord said, 'I will wipe mankind, whom I have created, from the face of the earth – men and animals, and creatures that move along the ground, and birds of the air – for I am grieved that I have made them.' But Noah found favor in the eyes of the LORD."

God chose to exhibit the reality of His divine justice because of wickedness. Evil always destroys; it is the absence of God's goodness. We ought to be thankful that God demonstrates how serious is the disease of sin and evil, for it inevitably and ultimately brings death (Romans 6:23). We are mistaken to believe that Noah was spared this judgment simply because He was obedient or a "good man." No man or woman is good by nature; we are sinners. There is no amount of good we can do and no proper way in which we can perform that earns the favor of God. We are very selfish by nature and – without the power of Jesus – quite capable of horrible evil.

Let me demonstrate that it was not the inherent goodness of Noah that saved him. If we remember when the flood subsided and Noah and his family were finally able to exit the ark, there were eight people in existence: Noah, his wife, his three sons, and his sons' wives. These eight people – Noah and his family – put their feet on the ground and then Noah built an altar. The Bible tells us, "Then Noah built an altar to the LORD and, taking some of all the clean animals and clean birds, he sacrificed burnt offerings on it. The LORD smelled the pleasing aroma and said in his heart: 'Never again will I curse the ground because of man, even though every inclination of his heart is evil from childhood" (Genesis 8:20-21a, NIV).

Just look at that description of the only eight people in existence on earth at the time: "every inclination of his heart is evil from childhood." This description sounds very familiar to the one God gave of all humanity before He sent the flood! Yes, even Noah was a sinner by nature; even Noah had evil inclination. We ask then, what was the difference? Why did God spare Noah if he was just as much a sinner by nature as all the other people who were destroyed by the flood?

The answer is found in Genesis 8:20-21. If you read those verses above again, you will notice that Noah built an altar and offered a burnt offering immediately after exiting the ark. It was the pleasing aroma of the sacrifice that prompted God to say that He would not destroy the earth in this way again despite man's nature. Why would the burning flesh of an animal please God? These Old Testament offerings were pictures, or a foreshadowing, of the soon-to-come offering of Jesus Christ Himself for the sin of mankind. Noah knew God, and he knew the promises of God. Noah believed that the Messiah would come, and he offered this burnt offering in faith. He was looking ahead to the coming of Jesus! Noah was demonstrating his belief in Jesus as the One who can appease God the Father and bring us into relationship with our Creator.

Jesus was Noah's salvation! Self-righteousness, good character, or self-effort could not save Noah or us. Only the sacrifice of Jesus Christ, His death and resurrection, can save a man or woman from sin and death. Noah looked forward and believed that Jesus would come. We look backward and believe that Jesus did come. Thank God, both we and Noah look ahead to the Second Coming of that same God-Man, Jesus Christ, when, as Hebrews 9:28 proclaims, He will appear with full salvation. We will then enjoy the new heavens and new earth, a home of righteousness.

Make no mistake about it, though, Noah's belief in Jesus Christ sent him into action! Because of his belief, Noah was willing to do God's will. He, no doubt, paid a dear price for building that ark. He and his family worked day in and day out doing God's will in a rebellious world. His belief prompted real action. In fact, real belief in Jesus Christ always prompts action; there is no other way to believe.

More than We Can Imagine

Now to him who is able to do immeasurably more than all we ask or imagine,
according to his power that is at work within us. . .

Ephesians 3:20 (NIV)

A trampoline is a load of fun. Of course I am talking about the big trampolines with protective netting around the sides. It would be an understatement to say that I jumped quite vigorously in one with my nephews recently.

Does projecting yourself vertically many feet into the air and landing in an "Indian style" sitting position, only to shoot right back up on both feet in the same bounce sound like vigorous trampoline work? Well, repeat that motion time and time again without stop. Then, add two little boys to the situation who ask you constantly to "bounce them higher" by forcing *yourself* to jump higher and harder. This is the stuff of trampoline heaven.

During one of my stints on that trampoline, I remember a distinct thought as my body rose into the air, enabling me to nearly brush the leaves of the surrounding trees. It was a beautiful day, and the feeling of nearly flying beneath the sunshine brought to mind a point from Ephesians 3:20 (NIV): God's ability to do immeasurably more than all we can imagine – according to His power working in us.

As a type I diabetic of twenty-eight years, I am thankful to Jesus for His sustaining, healing power in my body. By His grace, I have been active and have exercised most of my life. And, although I will suffer great soreness after being on that trampoline, I was exhilarated by the feeling of every part of my body – every muscle – being used to propel me up and all about. It felt like freedom. You cannot help but laugh while you are jumping like that, and you cannot help but feel like you are young all over again – like you have the world by the tail.

While bouncing in that silly trampoline, God reminded me that we do have the world by the tail! We are free. I want God to use every part of my life for His glory. I want to be totally spent for Him. How good it felt to have every muscle and joint used to "fly" yesterday. How good it feels to have every thought of our mind, every emotion of our heart, and every movement of our body used up by God; that is freedom.

It is hard for me to imagine that I can jump like I did. I know that someday soon I won't be able to do that in the same way. Sometimes it is also difficult for us to imagine that God could move through us mightily. But here is the key: God is able to do immeasurably more than what we can even imagine!

So get on the trampoline of life and let God use every part of you, while we wait for the day our resurrected bodies will literally jump again too!

Malfunctioning Horror Reflex

Have nothing to do with fruitless deeds of darkness, but rather expose them.
Ephesians 5:11 (NIV)

Driving down a road in my neighborhood after dark in late October, I was shocked by a sight that forced me to turn around and take another look. The light of the room behind a window in a house made the silhouette I saw stand out rather oddly. Against a big, living room window, I saw the outline of a cat sprawled out across the window screen from top to bottom. The cat appeared to be hanging on to the screen by its paws, and it seemed its fur was standing on end in all directions. The sight of the spread eagle, ter- rified cat caught my attention.

My first reaction was to assume the disturbing silhouette was a Halloween decoration, for most of the houses in the neighborhood were adorned with a myriad of frightful trimmings: witches riding broomsticks, witches crashing into front doors, skeletons hanging from trees, decaying arms and legs reaching from the ground, tombstones near front doors, giant spider webs on siding, ghosts and goblins floating in yards, and the like. Naturally, my mind had to wonder if this very odd sight was just part of the Halloween décor. What were the chances that an actual pet cat was hanging for dear life to the screen of a window on the outside of a house? Would it not be much more likely that during the fall season this was part of someone's "festive" Halloween practice?

I turned around because I wanted to be sure this was not an actual cat in danger. If it were, I wanted to help. Amazingly, as I drove past a second time, I saw a young girl reaching for a cat that was now halfway down the screen to the windowsill! A house- hold cat really did – somehow – manage to get stuck outside the house on a large, second floor window. Strange as it was, that feline sprawled out and clinging for dear life was a real cat. Its fur really had been standing on end. It actually had been in danger.

54

I nearly discounted the danger because of the prevalence of Halloween decorations. During these few weeks in late October, I am so accustomed to odd and gruesome sights that I almost did not take an actual, horrifying situation seriously.

Ephesians 5:11 (NIV) says, "Have nothing to do with fruitless deeds of darkness, but rather expose them." I fear that we as Christians have grown too accustomed to comfort with sin. We are so willingly exposed to things with which we ought to have nothing to do. We regularly get too close to selfishness, greed, indecent television shows, graphic language, gossip, bitter hearts, godless philosophy, etc. Our refusal to obey Ephesians 5:11 has left us in a place where we are no longer horrified when we should be.

And so the enemy proceeds in slicing away at our vitality. Sometimes we Christians begin to think we are invincible. We are not. These fruitless deeds of darkness are in our own "spiritual neighborhood" – our houses, our hearts, our social circles. Prolonged exposure – which is, by the way, rebellion against God's Word – leaves us confused and unable to react as we ought. Our "horror reflex" is not activated as it should be. Sin begins to creep into every corner, with all its nasty consequences.

Had I seen the spread eagle cat on the window screen in the month of April, I most likely would have never doubted the immediate danger the cat was in. It was the proliferation of appalling sights at Halloween that made me hesitate.

Dear Lord, please keep me far from fruitless deeds of darkness. May I be so accustomed to Your light and Your truth – and so uncomfortable with sin in and around my life – that I react quickly to the horror that rebellion against You brings.

Darkness Dispelled

Even the darkness is not dark to You, And the night is as bright as the day.
Darkness and light are alike to You.

Psalm139:12

In the darkest of nights
And the brightest of days,

God is at work all the while.

No candle He needs,
No fumbling about,

Though murky and deep be the trial.

For God is light,
So where He is

The way stands clear and sure.

We yet perceive darkness
As we struggle with sin,

But God's view of things is most pure.

Light chases darkness until it is gone,
Dispelling confusion and fear.

In an instant,
A beam cuts through shadowy night,
And suddenly things become clear.

In a moment,
Jesus charges through all space and time,
And swiftly our answers are near.

Troubled by the Tribulation

So Christ was sacrificed once to take away the sins of many people; and he will
appear a second time, not to bear sin, but to bring salvation
to those who are waiting for him.

Hebrews 9:28 (NIV)

Recently a group of second grade students at Christian school was very much troubled by the tribulation. Some had become fixated on the number "666" as their little minds pondered the end times. A few had actually become afraid of the devil's work as the day of Christ's return approaches.

As a principal who loved my students and loves the Word of God, I was happy to visit the classroom personally and attempt – by God's Holy Spirit – to calm these precious souls. I emphasized three basic points for these adorable, inquisitive kids: 1) the reality of God's power and control, 2) the reason for Jesus' Second Coming for Christians, and 3) the status of heart Jesus wants us to have regarding the end of time.

I found the reiteration of these basic, Biblical principles did me a world of good! I hope a brief discussion of each vital concept will lift your heart today.

1) The reality of God's power and control.

Question: Who made God?
Answer: No one.
Follow-up: No one made God because He is the biggest and most powerful. He had no beginning, and no one can stop Him or His plan!

Question: Who made Satan?
Answer: God.

Follow-up: Though first created as an angel of light, the devil is only a created being. Therefore, He is nothing compared to God, His Creator. He is no match for Jesus in any way, shape, or form! (Even in the desperation of the end times.)

2) **The reason for Jesus' second coming for Christians (based on Hebrews 9:28)**.

Question: Why did Jesus come the first time to Earth?
Answer: To take away our sins.

Question: Why is Jesus coming back the second time?
Answer: To rescue us!
Follow-up: We are forgiven because Jesus came to Earth the first time to bear our sins on the cross. When He comes the second time, he will rescue us from all of sin's effects and influence. In the Greek, the word for "salvation" here is equated to "deliverance" or "rescue." Jesus is coming back to make us completely safe! No more will we battle sin, no more will people hurt one another, no more will anyone be sick or die.

3) **The status of heart Jesus wants us to have regarding the end of time**.

Question: What is the first thing Jesus said when he began to tell His disciples about the world He is preparing for us?
Answer: "Do not let your heart be troubled." (John 14:1)
Follow-up: When we think about the New Heaven and the New Earth that Jesus is making for us, we ought to do so with a heart that is untroubled. Though Jesus has left Earth for now, He wants us to know that He is completely trust-worthy. He made this world and all its glorious contents, and He is making the next world. The difference is that the world to come will be perfect and complete because God will have His way unhindered there! In the meantime, do not become unduly focused on the details of the end of time. Rather,

become intently focused on the God of all power, Who is returning to rescue us, and Who wants us to be untroubled in the meantime.

May this response to a second grade concern comfort our adult hearts. God's Word is beautiful in its simplicity for all.

Who Is God's Favorite?

For this finds favor, if for the sake of conscience toward God a person bears up under sorrows when suffering unjustly . . . but if when you do what is right and suffer for it you patiently endure it, this finds favor with God.

I Peter 2:19-20

Students always envy the "teacher's pet." Siblings tease about who is mom's favorite. Employees long to be "in good" with the boss. Why? Clearly, teachers wield moderate power in the educational context, parents have a tremendous impact during our growing-up years, and supervisors definitely influence our professional lives. But, would you not love to be a favorite of God?

God is sovereign over every realm. Now, I understand that being the teacher's pet has fleeting advantages, and promotions may come easier when the boss has high regard for us; but what are the infinite privileges of rapport with the One who owns galaxies, causes flowers to bloom, provides breath to all people, and decides just when and how to close out this chapter of human history and usher in a perfect world? I want an advantage with Him for sure!

Hold onto your hat, because favor with God comes in a way you might not expect . . . bearing up under suffering for doing the right thing! "For this finds favor, if for the sake of conscience toward God a person bears up under sorrows when suffering unjustly . . . but if when you do what is right and suffer for it you patiently endure it, this finds favor with God" (I Peter 2:19-20). And there it is — simple, but not so glamorous. Straightforward and rock-solid, but not fitting the appetite of this culture. No matter, for we know the One who transcends the ebb and flow of civilization, the One who fashioned our souls with His own hands and understands that our heart's real need is His approval.

Therefore, stand strong. Do right. Do not sway in the midst of fervent attack against virtue. Though the fury of Hell comes against your soul and even brothers turn to enemies, be not dissuaded from acting rightly. Allow no excuse for sinful reaction. Though you are mistreated, neglected, ostracized, and castigated for doing what God calls you to do; persevere with your mind fixed on Christ and your heart wholly yielded to God.

Of two things you can consequently be sure: His Spirit will fuel your arduous journey, and the favor of the Maker and Sustainer of the universe will rest on you. No one can imagine what glorious reward awaits the person who is favored by the One who tells both galaxies and electrons what to do!

Against All Odds

Declaring the end from the beginning, And from ancient times things which have not been done, Saying, "My purpose will be established, And I will accomplish all My good pleasure"

Isaiah 46:10

For various reasons, it can be difficult at times for people to keep their word. Additionally, people sometimes refuse to keep their word even though they could. Our culture has seemingly grown a generation of people who barely know what it means to be a "person of your word." It seems the days are gone when a simple handshake insures a promise kept.

Despite the instability of human nature, I assure you that God keeps His Word. Given the nature of His being, it is impossible for God to change or go back on His Word. For God to be God, He must be perfect. For Him to change His mind or go back on His Word would mean He could somehow possibly improve through a change. God cannot improve. He is infinite and holy. If you posit anything other than a perfect God, you no longer have God. You have someone or something less than our true, self-sustaining, perfect God.

The God of the Bible keeps His Word. We observe that He has kept His Word against all odds throughout history to date. Namely, Jesus has already fulfilled approximately three hundred prophecies concerning Him. I will give just two examples. As I describe the examples, bear in mind that the Bible is not really one book. It is, in fact, a collection of sixty-six books written over a period of 1,500 years by more than forty human authors on three continents and in three languages. This is a vital fact to remember when we discuss fulfilled prophecy.

Micah, the prophet, wrote circa 700 B.C. He prophesied the Messiah would be born in the obscure town of Bethlehem (Micah

5:2). Jesus was born in Bethlehem in the first century A.D. (Matthew 2:1-7). This prophetic detail proved accurate, though the span of time between prediction and fulfillment was 750 or more years. David prophesied in Psalm 22:16 that the Messiah would be crucified. Though crucifixion did not yet exist at the time of David's writing (circa 1000 B.C.), the prophecy was fulfilled more than one thousand years later!

The examples above are just two of many that could be mentioned. Keep in mind how difficult it is to predict details of the distant future. If I were to predict rain tomorrow and you actually encountered raindrops, you might not consider me too amazing. However, if I were to predict rain on the afternoon of April 12 in the year 2053 and it actually happened, you might say, "Wow! Shelli is amazing!" But what if I correctly predicted rain on April 12, 2053, in a 12.5 mile radius of Greensburg, Pennsylvania, at exactly 4:09 in the afternoon for seven minutes and thirty-two seconds? Then you might proclaim, "That Shelli has supernatural ability!" In other words, the more details I add and the longer the time frame spanned, the more difficult – against the odds – the correct prediction of the future becomes.

The God of the Bible has made more than three hundred detailed prophecies concerning His Son, Jesus Christ, which have already come true. Lee Strobel has nicely outlined in his book, *The Case for Christ (Student Edition)*, the findings of Dr. Peter Stoner. Dr. Stoner and some of his students worked to calculate the mathematical probability of fulfilled prophecy. It has been estimated that the probability of Jesus fulfilling in His earthly lifetime just eight of the Biblical prophecies about Him is one in 10^{17}. That is a chance of one in one hundred million billion! To better visualize these astronomical odds, picture the following scenario.

Pretend that we cover the surface of the entire earth with 1.5 inch square tiles. We cover not just the state of Wyoming with these small tiles – not just the land surface of North America – but we coat every inch of land on the entire planet. We decide at the outset to mark the underside of just *one* of these tiles with a gold star. Then, much to his chagrin, we send a young man out to roam the seven continents for the rest of life. As he nears one hundred years old, we ask him to bend over – wherever he now happens to be located – and pick up one of the tiles. The chance of him selecting the only tile marked with a gold star is one in one hundred million billion!

As you begin to grasp by the above example, the chance of Jesus fulfilling just eight of the prophecies about Him defies all odds. Consider the chance of Him fulfilling forty-eight prophecies grows to a staggering one in 10^{157}! This would be like choosing one particular electron out of all the known electrons in all the known mass of the universe! God certainly keeps His Word *against all odds*.

As if all of this is not exciting enough, we now use God's track record to remind ourselves that He will *continue* to keep His Word against all odds. Despite the daily routine of life and all its problems, despite the fact that so many people cannot possibly believe it's true, and despite the fact that even many Christians do not consider it a vital part of everyday thinking; God will keep His Word about the second coming of Jesus just as He has kept His Word on Jesus' first coming to earth. The three hundred prophecies that have already been fulfilled by Jesus' first invasion into space and time inspire us to know that He is coming back again to fulfill all the Bible's truth!

Here is one thing God has told us about Jesus that we are yet to see: "For the Lord himself will come down from heaven, with a loud command, with the voice of the archangel and with the trumpet call of God, and the dead in Christ will rise first. After that, we who are still alive and are left will be caught up together with them in the clouds to meet the Lord in the air. And so we will be with the Lord forever" (I Thessalonians 4:16-17, NIV). Can you even imagine this scene? Thank God for the day when we will rise with new, glorified bodies to be with our Lord in the New Heavens and New Earth!

Does this sound too good to be true? Remember, God fulfills His Word though it seems impossible.

Or how about the fact that God has promised the following historical event? "Look, he [Jesus] is coming with the clouds, and every eye will see him, even those who pierced him; and all the peoples of the earth will mourn because of him. So shall it be! Amen. I [Jesus] am the Alpha and the Omega, says the Lord God, 'who is, and who was, and who is to come, the Almighty'" (Revelation 1:7-8, NIV).

If God has kept His Word against all odds — and if He is perfect and immutable (changeless) — then certainly He will keep His Word now and in the future. I trust today the God who said in the first century A.D., "Never will I leave you; never will I forsake you" (Hebrews 13:5b, NIV).

Do you believe in the God of the Bible? Pour over Isaiah chapter forty. Refresh your confidence in God's unchanging and holy nature. If He is truly God, then He can do nothing other than keep His Word. History and mathematics demonstrate His ability beyond the natural realm to be faithful to His promises. Trust Him for today and tomorrow, for He has a proven track record!

Are You Desperate?

A blind man, Bartimaeus (that is, the Son of Timaeus), was sitting by the roadside begging. When he heard that it was Jesus of Nazareth, he began to shout, "Jesus, Son of David, have mercy on me!" Many rebuked him and told him to be quiet, but he shouted all the more, "Son of David, have mercy on me!" Jesus stopped and said, "Call him."

Mark 10:46b-49a (NIV)

A blind man who had to beg in order to live calls out to Jesus from the roadside. Only, he does not just call – he cries out loudly. The Greek word behind the description is the same word used for the call of a raven. This man is obviously unafraid of the reaction of others. He is most desperate; He wants his life to be changed, and he recognizes as the Messiah this Jesus from the simple town of Nazareth.

Bartimaeus heard that the man walking down his road was Jesus, and Bartimaeus' entire paradigm shifted. No more would he look to the crowds around him for sustenance as he begged pitifully from them. Bartimaeus – upon hearing the name of Jesus – realizes that the hope he had formerly pinned on the pity of others needed to be targeted on the one Man, Jesus Christ.

Though the crowd sharply rebuked blind Bartimaeus for his interruption, his loud annoyance, his audacity; Bartimaeus cried out all the louder to Jesus. The blind man was smart enough to know that the crowd was not his concern any longer, though he had to this point depended on them for physical sustenance. Bartimaeus wisely decided that he needed Jesus, no matter the cost or embarrassing measures to reach Him.

What about us? In a society that teaches us to be refined, measured, and unduly concerned with the thoughts of others; have we ceased to cry out to Jesus as we ought? Has our Savior walked down the road right beside us, but for fear of looking too dependent on

Him, have we let Him walk by? Has Jesus stood near – longing to intervene and meet our deepest needs – but we have been too proud to demonstrate our heart's desperation for Him?

Cry out! Do not allow a classy culture or a too-refined people stop you from calling out to the only One whose mercy can change everything. Let others see that you need Jesus, that you believe He is your only hope, and that you are not ashamed to admit that you are nothing without Him.

When Bartimaeus shouted the second time – despite the discouragement of others – Jesus actually stopped in His tracks! Our Savior paused and told His disciples to summon the blind beggar. Bartimaeus threw off his coat and literally jumped to his feet when he realized the Messiah – the anointed One of God – heard the cry of a broken heart. And then, Jesus poured out His mercy on Bartimaeus; Jesus restored the sight that had been lost.

What is your need that the mercy of Jesus requires? What sight have you lost? The sight of a clean heart, the sight of a hope after death, the sight of peace during troubled times, the sight of a healed body, the sight of a clear mind?

Call out to Jesus with all your heart, no matter who hears, and no matter what they think. Show by your words and actions that you need the Savior more than you need anything else. He will pause, and He will restore your sight.

The Answer for the Living Dead

For you have delivered my soul from death, yes, my feet from falling, that I may walk before God in the light of life.

Psalm 56:15 (ESV)

Ultimately, people want to live — truly live. This is quite natural, given that our Creator breathed into humanity the breath of life at the beginning of time. Sadly, many people who live biologically are inwardly dead. Their lungs are taking in air, and their hearts are beating; but their spirits are dead with the weight of sadness, guilt, hopelessness, futility, and fear. Medical doctors can work on the body, but it takes an infinitely better Physician to work on the spirit.

The ancient — yet timeless — book of Psalms outlines the process of coming to realize the vitality of genuine living. The writer says of God, "For you have delivered my soul from death, yes, my feet from falling, that I may walk before God in the light of life" (Psalm 56:13, ESV). Here we observe three critical components of a life of vitality.

1) **God delivers the soul from death.** No matter how our pride may fight against this truth, it takes God to deliver a soul from death. The wages of our sin brings death — first spiritual, and eventually physical (Romans 6:23). No slick mental tricks or serious psychological manipulation can erase the guilt of a heart in rebellion against the God of the Bible. Once we come to terms with our sinful heart by the conviction of God's own Spirit, we can ask God to give us life by making our heart new through the sacrifice of Jesus Christ. His blood which was shed on the Cross pays for the guilt of my sin, and His life (evidenced by the Resurrection) provides life to me. *Here it is again: His blood pays, and His life provides.*

2) **God delivers our feet from falling.** Simply amazing is the provision of God for the daily minutes and hours of life. Not

only has He given vitality to my soul by the forgiveness of sins and restoration of life, He promises to keep my feet from falling as I walk through this world on a regular basis. This portion of Scripture gets down to the nitty-gritty!

Real living – beyond the basics of biology – requires the security of knowing that we are being guided and protected by the One who can assure the outcome. Each moment of each day, we can depend on our Savior to keep our feet from falling – into demise, hopelessness, and trial outside the will of God. We can even rely on our Savior to provide what we need in order that we will not fall into sin. Though as humans we will not be perfect until we finally see Jesus face-to-face; there exists no excuse for our sin, because God can deliver our feet from falling.

3) God allows me to walk before Him in the light of life.

Here it is – the culmination of real living. Darkness of soul is gone, and we can live our moments before the face of God without dread. We know that we stand clean before Him because of Jesus, and there is no need to hide. We can now truly relate to others, for we are walking in the transparency of God's light.

For those God has delivered, death is swallowed up in victory (I Corinthians 15:54b). Not only can we live before Him with hope now, we know that we will live forever before Him in glory that cannot be fully understood or described this side of eternity.

Do not allow death to stay. Do not allow life to pass you by. Let God deliver you.

Quite the Opposite of a Cop-out

> But I said, "I have toiled in vain, I have spent My strength for nothing and vanity; yet surely the justice due to Me is with the LORD,
> And My reward with My God.
>
> Isaiah 49:4

I believe the first rule of genuine Christian leadership is a precept some may label a cop-out. God does not classify it this way; God describes this principle as truth. Here is the rule: Your reward is secure with God and will not be fully realized this side of eternity. Corollary to the rule: You will at times feel exhausted and discouraged, but these are only feelings; the truth remains unassailable.

Isaiah 49:4 proclaims, "But I said, 'I have toiled in vain, I have spent My strength for nothing and vanity; yet surely the justice due to Me is with the LORD, and My reward with My God.'" Interestingly, the prophet Isaiah has done here something for which he is known well. He is speaking generally to the people of his time, but He is also speaking specifically of the Messiah. As it is true of Jesus, so it is true of His servants. We grow weary from all the fury Hell can bring and we grow disheartened from all the loneliness of leadership and its unique responsibility. And yet again, as it is with Jesus, so it is with us. The Father promises to do right in the end. The sovereign Lord is working His plan, and He will bring the reward swiftly and surely.

Do you ever have days where the phrases "toiled in vain" and "spent My strength for nothing" seem all too familiar? If we are only focusing on what we can see with our eyeballs right now, we will no doubt feel empty at times. However, if we focus on a reward currently invisible but nonetheless tangible, we will grasp the sense of the phrase, "*surely* the justice due to Me is with the Lord, and My reward with My God."

I am not sure why it is that at times even Christians give into the perception of "pie in the sky stuff" when it comes to belief in a reward in another world. I think part of the reason is a culture foolishly enamored with a definition of success realized by numbers, profit, and popularity. Standing in stark contrast to the belief of many, a reason that God says He is not ashamed of us is that we "desire a better country, that is, a heavenly one" (Hebrews 11:16). Imagine – God is proud of us for desiring the reality of Heaven! This verse does not proclaim God's pride in us for what we achieve or desire here and now, but He is proud when we desire our heavenly home and all its reward and glory.

Though all human accolade be withheld, we shall yet stand before God and be delighted by the faces of those who have been greatly or even remotely affected by our service to Jesus Christ. They heard one word we spoke, they watched one godly reaction of ours, they felt our Savior's love through our hug, they observed a life of passion for eternal things, they benefitted from our offering to the work of God, they heard of Jesus from the friend of a friend of a friend of someone with whom we shared the Gospel, or they lived out their life in close proximity to ours as we served the living God.

Though we be misunderstood, unappreciated, maligned, forgotten, or persecuted; our reward is with our God. Peter says of that inheritance, "[it is] reserved in heaven for you" (I Peter 1:4). No small matter is it that the reward is also imperishable, undefiled, and will not fade away. Discouragement cannot tarnish our reward, economic downturn cannot diminish our reward, human evil cannot debase our reward, and time cannot corrode our reward. No human may ever fully understand what we have done, are doing, or will do. But, God knows. Our labor for Him is not in vain.

Do you want to be a leader? First and foremost, know where your reward is. The chances of survival in leadership are nil if you are counting on anything other than the living God for your strength and satisfaction.

Only Two Options

For the Lord watches over the way of the righteous, but the way of
the wicked will perish.

Psalm1:6 (NIV)

"I'd rather die than be watched all the time." Really? Think it through because those are the only two options. No kidding. There exist only two ways a person can live: in alignment with God's will or out of alignment with God's will. And let me tell you, God's will is going to prevail. God's way is the only way that lasts, and I will explain shortly.

"For the Lord *watches over* the way of the righteous, but the way of the wicked will perish" (Psalm 1:6, NIV, emphasis mine). There it is. Black and white. Straightforward. One way – that of righteous-ness – is watched over. The other way – that of the unrighteous – is destroyed. If you think about it, the reason is simple enough. I mean, even now, we see God's natural law (His way of working in this natural world) operating constantly, tirelessly, and relentlessly:

- The law of gravity, for example, always wins out over my rebellion against it. (I wish someone would have told me that when I was five years old and tried to fly!)
- The laws of logic and mathematics are the statutes according to which we must construct massive buildings and expansive bridges if we wish them to be safe. (Jeremiah 33:25)
- The laws of planetary motion continue on – night and day – producing the natural rhythm of seasons and days. (Genesis 8:22)

The dependable nature of God's natural law hints to us of the impeccable reliability of His spiritual law! Jesus once said to a seeker, "I have spoken to you of earthly things and you do not believe; how then will you believe if I speak to you of heavenly things?" (John 3:12, NIV)

God's moral law is right because it is the way He intended things to be. His "watching over our way" is our **hope**, not our threat! When I live according to the Bible by the power of God's Spirit, it will go well for me now and perfectly for me in the next world. All rebellion against God's way ends in ultimate misery. Turning against God begins to make things messy. Then – finally – one day Jesus will come back to clean up the mess of sin and make a home of righteousness that works right and feels right because it is right!

It is not only the wicked who perish; it is the whole way of the wicked. If that way of living lasted forever, things would never be right.

It is not only the righteous that God watches over; it is the way of the righteous. Since that way will ultimately prevail, I want to be carefully watched and helped in that way presently.

If you need to find that Way, His name is Jesus. Please let Him save you and watch you. It is an understatement to say that the alternative is bleak.

The Glorious Remaking

The sacrifices of God are a broken spirit; a broken and contrite heart,
O God, You will not despise.

Psalm 51:17

I gave to You a heart burdened with my own sin,
But I gave it to You;
And You made it a clean heart, free of guilt and shame.

I gave to You a mind shackled by fear,
But I gave it to You;
And You made it a strong mind, focused on truth.

I gave to You hands prone to selfishness and greed,
But I gave them to You;
And You made them hands extended, inclined to reach out.

I gave to You a will fixed on my own plans,
But I gave it to You;
And You made it a will to love You, unshaken by changing
  circumstance.

I gave to You the moments of my life, not seeming to amount
  to much as the second hand ticks so relentlessly,
But I gave them to You;
And You made them moments of eternal weight, reaching
  infinitely far into the future.

I gave to You my dreams, so elusive and unreal,
But I gave them to You;
And You made them dreams aligned with Your plan, bursting
  into glorious reality.

I gave to You my future, which is – without You – nothing,
But I gave it to you;
And You made it a future never-ending, always glorious.

I gave to You me, though I cannot add one bit to Your
    greatness;
But I gave me to You;
And You made me who I always wanted to be – the person You
    want me to be.

Your Relationship with Jesus:
Formality or Reality

Behold I stand at the door and knock; if anyone hears my voice and opens the door, I will come in to him and will dine with him, and he with Me.
Revelation 3:20

Have you ever been out to lunch with someone for business purposes, or for some other obligation? The fellow diner is not someone with whom you feel very comfortable. And so you provide obligatory conversation, eat very carefully – obeying all the formal dining rules – and wonder if the impression you emit is quite satisfactory. On these somewhat nerve-wracking occasions, you discover that even your favorite pasta dish is not as mouthwatering as usual. Your smile strains your facial muscles, instead of hearty laughter erupting from your gut.

On the other hand, the steak seems juicier, the conversation flows freely, and laughter is unbridled at the dinner table of two real friends. When genuine companions get together, the dining is sweet because the dining is real, built on the comfort of relationship.

Jesus said in Revelation 3:20, "Behold I stand at the door and knock; if anyone hears My voice and opens the door, I will come in to him and will dine with him, *and he with Me*" (emphasis mine). Why did Jesus add those last four words? Why did He not just leave it at "I will dine with you"? At the surface, it seems redundant to say it both ways: "I will dine with you *and* you will dine with Me." But God does not waste words! He added the vital second part because real dining – the kind of dining you want to do – involves not just a guest and a host, but two people in relationship.

When Jesus spoke these pointed words, He was addressing a group of people whose love for God had grown cold, formal, and religious. God despises religion, but adores relationship. And so, our Savior proclaims, "Be zealous and repent" in order that you may invite Me in to eat with you and truly enjoy My company.

Do you enjoy your relationship with Jesus? Or has religious formality crept in as the busyness of your life rages on? Pray now. Pray sincerely. Be real. Tell Jesus you are sorry that He and you are not connecting at the core. Then invite Him in to dine with you *and you with Him*.

A Teacher's Reflection

A God of faithfulness . . .

Deuteronomy 32:4

The job of a teacher is mysteriously all-pervasive. A real educator touches not only things academic, but things emotional, psychological, and spiritual. A teacher has a profound task as he demonstrates his life – not simply his brain – to all his students each and every day. Successful teachers are simply amazing, and their work's difficulty is commensurate with its importance.

Perseverance is a hallmark attribute of the world's best educators. A dedicated teacher considers the daily sacrifice required to give of oneself on so many levels, and the dedicated teacher decides the sacrifice is well worth it.

God told us in His Word that He is a "God of faithfulness" (Deuteronomy 32:4). I believe true teachers – in the right and Biblical sense of the word – beautifully reflect this critical attribute of God, His faithfulness.

To those among us who diligently plan lessons into the wee hours of the morning, who rise early to meet tired faces, who stay late to tutor the confused, who stand on their feet many hours in front of a myriad of young minds, whose fingers are stained by day's end with ink and dry erase markers, whose homes are filled with textbooks and notebooks, whose many evening hours are spent reviewing the work of the day, whose mouths are dry before lunchtime ever arrives, whose brains ache for being pulled in so many directions at once, whose heads are filled with plans to improve, and whose hearts overflow with love for those who are tomorrow's hope; know this: you reflect the faithfulness of our God.

Though your days are both rewarding and wearisome, rejoice that you have been called to be as God is, faithful. Our Creator stands by His people through thick and thin, with patience unending. Our Creator does not abandon His people when they fail. Our Creator sees the best in His own. He strives and strives with His children at unimaginable cost.

Teacher, hold on to the high calling that is yours. Your own resources are limited, but your God's resources are not. Our faithfulness falls short, but His is perfect. You exhibit His tenacity in your daily work. And when you grow weary, remember that you not only *reflect* His faithfulness; you *have* His faithfulness on which to depend.

Healed Bruises

. . .to set at liberty them that are bruised.

Luke 4:18b (KJV)

Bruises hurt. The soreness of a significant bruise on my right wrist may cause me to be very careful about using my arm for a few days. I may become apt to slow down, be too cautious, and miss out on activity because of the tenderness.

The Bible tells us that Jesus came "to set at liberty them that are bruised" (Luke 4:18b, KJV). We humans get bruised spiritually in this life. While physical bruises are ruptured blood vessels resulting in pain that can cause hesitation, spiritual bruises are hearts broken by sin's effects. These bruises of the heart can stultify our emotional lives and compel debilitating cautiousness. Whether we read in the King James Version of the freedom bruised ones receive, or we read in the New International Version of the release of the oppressed, the Greek word implies that we are broken, shattered, and blown to pieces in a spiritual sense.

Jesus came to free us from the effects of sin's bruising. Do you feel stifled by the guilt of your past? Are you hesitant to enter into God's plan for your life because of sin's effects? There is no bruising effect from which Jesus cannot set us free!

Some spiritual bruising is the result of our own rebellion against God's righteousness. Some bruising comes because we suffer under the general effects of sin: broken relationships, illness and disease, disabilities, economic hardship, emotional weaknesses passed down through generations, and dozens of other agonies.

Know this: "Jesus came to set at liberty them that are bruised." His shed blood and resurrection from death provide the healing for our bruises. Please do not allow the enemy to steal from you the glory of moving forward each day in God's plan without hesitation:

Our past will not stifle us.
Our former failures cannot make us stagger.
Our undeserved heartache will not command dawdling.
Our suffering bodies will not make us tentative.

We are resolute and ready to pursue every dream and purpose God has for us. Why? Because Jesus has set us free from life's bruising effects.

Self-Deception vs. Doing Right

Every man's way is right in his own eyes, but the LORD weighs the hearts. To do righteousness and justice is desired by the LORD more than sacrifice.
Proverbs 21:2-3

How easy it is to convince ourselves we are right. How often we try to persuade our hearts that we are the people we ought to be. If each human being were the one responsible for determining right and wrong for himself or herself, we would be in a mess most miserable.

I think of times when I have worked hard to tell myself that I was doing the right thing. What I really longed for was an excuse – a way to get out of doing the difficult work of righteousness and justice. And every single time I refuse to do right – whether justified in my own mind or not – someone somewhere gets hurt. The ripple effect of unrighteousness is occasionally obvious and at times hidden. It may be ten or twenty or one hundred people down the line from my injustice that finally feel the pain of that selfishness. One thing is for sure, when we do not live justly, pain will ensue. How do I know? I see it experientially in everyday living, and God has made it clear in His Word that His way of righteousness is how things were meant to be. Rebellion against the Creator's way always brings heartbreak, for He is the Designer of how things ought to be.

Proverbs 21:2 makes clear that though we may convince ourselves we are right, God Almighty weighs our hearts. There is a transcendent God who sees us for who we really are. He is not swayed by our persuasive rhetoric and excessive pride. He knows what we are really about. His assessment comes from the outside – from the unbiased perspective of perfection – and He will assess rightly.

This transcendent God has said in Proverbs 21:3 that "to do righteousness and justice is desired by the Lord more than sacrifice." Wow. The offering of sacrifice in the Old Testament was the heart of the "church" in that day. Is God implying that the action of doing right is more important than pretentious church activity? Remember the context is the deception of one's own heart for selfish reasons. Yes, it is more important to actually do right as God has commanded than to try to feel right by performing out-ward "religious" actions that we think will compensate for our disobedience.

My friends, nothing will compensate for a heart that is bent to be unjust through its own self-deception, except for one thing: the sacrifice of Jesus Christ. The problem is that we have to actually quit trying to convince ourselves we are right long enough to admit we are a mess at the core, so that we can accept Jesus' sacrifice on our behalf.

Those who know the Lord Jesus Christ will do well to actually go about doing the hard stuff of righteousness and justice. We must quit playing the religious angle to excuse our refusal to hunker down and do right. It can be difficult to live with integrity. We must tell the truth, not allow the innocent to suffer if we can help, inter-vene when it is within our sphere of influence to correct injustice, protect others though it cost us our strength, work with those who have been pummeled by life though we do not see reward just yet, expose wicked plans that they may be thwarted, stand up for the ones who have not a voice to be heard, and love even when it hurts.

We must do more than think about our own hearts. We must yield them to our transcendent God for His inspection. We should allow His Holy Spirit to "weigh our hearts" to prevent self-decep-tion and its consequent unrighteousness. For, to actually do the formidable work of righteousness and justice is desired by the Lord more than sacrifice.

The Day the Earth Runs

*Then I saw a great white throne and him who was seated on it. Earth and sky
fled from his presence, and there was no place for them.*
Revelation 20:11 (NIV)

When a person is most sure of his conclusion, we may hear him
say, "I'm as sure as the ground I'm standin' on." To which I might
reply, "Really? Because the ground we are all standing on is not as
secure as you might think!"

Despite its relative smallness when compared to the vastness of
the known universe, earth is a pretty big deal to us. It is our planet.
The terrain feels solid beneath our feet. The power of its natural
laws keeps our activity within God-ordained boundaries. We have
a well-deserved respect for earth, such a mysterious place. And
though this orb may seem tiny compared to billions of galaxies, it is
quite overwhelming to the countless humans residing here.

However, the earth will one day have to flee. Revelation 20:11
makes clear, "Then I saw a great white throne and him who was
seated on it. Earth and sky fled from his presence, and there was
no place for them." Amazingly, this earth and the heavens surrounding are incredibly unstable when compared to their Maker.
When God steps to the throne as Judge, not even this miraculous
sphere will survive His magnificence. Earth and sky are suffering the
same conundrum that sinners are; they are on the path of ruination
because of sin. They must flee until the time of their remaking. All
things must be perfected for the people God has saved.

To be sure, the Great Architect – God Almighty – will perfect the
earth and heavens in keeping with His promise of a home of righteousness for His people (II Peter 3:12-13). The new Earth and New
Heavens will function properly: no disasters, no obstacles to harvest or discoveries, no killer species, no deadly or damaging virus,
and no decay.

The remaking will happen after the earth infused with sin has flown appropriately from its Holy Judge. God will deal with the old earth in His time. Therefore, I put no stock in this firm ground beneath my feet. As the old hymn rings out, "On Christ the Solid Rock I stand; all other ground is sinking sand." Or, shall we say, "Fleeing turf"?

Do not trust in anything but the Holy Judge who will ultimately destroy what is wrong and rebuild to make right. Earth seems dependable, but it will answer to God in the end. Put not your trust in what you see, but in the God who is unseen and infinitely greater than what He has made.

The question remains, how will I stand on that day when even the earth has to run? I will stand because – unlike earth and sky – I have already been remade! II Corinthians 5:17 (NIV) boldly declares, "Therefore, if anyone is in Christ, he is a new creation; the old has gone, the new has come!" The old earth flees, but I am already new in my spirit!

Take heart. The Bible says, "If *anyone* is in Christ. . ." Choose to be found in Christ today. Then – and *only* then – will your footing be sure.

Truly, Where Is Your Trust?

Then the LORD said to Moses, "Behold, I will rain bread from heaven for you;
and the people shall go out and gather a day's portion every day. . ."
Exodus 16:4

Just some weeks into the Israelites' adventure in the wilderness following their miraculous exodus from Egypt, God's people began grumbling against Moses and Aaron because they were hungry. Recall that these people had watched God send massive plagues (including the plague of death) to ensure their freedom from Pharoah, they had seen the application of blood over their doorposts stop the death angel cold in his tracks, and they had watched with mouths agape as God divided the sea in half for their safe pilgrimage. And still, the Israelites make the wrong assumption that God has brought them all this way to kill them (Exodus 16:3).

As they continue complaining about their hunger, I can only imagine God's thoughts. If I were God (and – wow – are we thankful I am not), I would have looked at the lot of them and said, "You ungrateful brats! Don't you see what I have done? Do you really believe I have rescued you to kill you?" Thankfully, this is not what God says. I, myself, am particularly grateful for this fact; for I am one of the ungrateful, unbelieving brats.

God answers their complaining doubt by saying, "Behold, I will rain bread from heaven for you" (Exodus 16:4). God is truly "something else," isn't He? It is truly all about Him. Even after I have trusted Him for salvation, I still fail. But God is faithful!

The detail we should highlight here is God's prescription for the manna. He told the Israelites to collect enough for each day, *one day at a time.* (Exodus 16:4) Throughout the week, they were to collect only enough for the day at hand and not stockpile it for the next day. Moses reiterated, "Let no man leave any of it until morning" (Exodus 16:19).

As we can imagine (because we know ourselves well), some of the people left manna from one day until the following morning. The results were very repulsive. The manna left over for the next day "bred worms and became foul" (Exodus 16:20). Smelly manna teeming with maggots is not what the Israelites had in mind! Yet, this was the result for those who tried to carry one day's portion into the next day.

The question becomes, "Why?" Why did God do this? The answer is clear and confirmed in many other portions of the Bible. *God wants us to trust Him and not ourselves and all our efforts.* People who hoarded the bread for the next day either did not believe God would rain down manna in the morning as He promised, or they did not believe God would give them strength the next day to go collect it. Either way, they did not trust the Living Lord.

My friends, He wants us to know that He will be there tomorrow morning with all the provision of food, strength, and sanity that we need. We are not to work by our own efforts to devise a way to survive; relationship with and trust in God is our only way to survive.

Jesus confirms this emphasis in the Gospel of John, Chapter 6. When large crowds cross a body of water to be with Him, He does not employ "seeker-friendly" techniques. He chastises the crowd by informing them that they have followed Him for the wrong reasons; they have only come because their hungry stomachs had been filled when He had performed the miracle with the fish and bread. Jesus proceeds to tell the crowd, "I am the living bread that came down out of heaven" (John 6:51a).

The crowd was into following Jesus because of His miracles that satisfied their fleshly desires. The people even brought up the miracle of manna in the wilderness of which we have been speaking (John 6:31). But Jesus was sure to emphasize that though the recipients of this manna had eaten it, they still died an earthly death. The physical manna was not the key. The key was and is trust in the God who gives the manna.

Jesus told the crowd He is the Living Bread. He is letting us know that we should trust the one who never sleeps, never gets ill, never gives up, and never dies. God is alive. God will be there in the morning when we awake to give to us everything we need to live the next day. Do not mistrust Him by trying on your own to make things work and trying to ensure your own destiny. Jesus is alive. If we trust Him, He will provide – one moment at a time.

Be sure of this, any plans or efforts employed outside of pure trust in Him will produce repulsive results, similar to the manna teeming with maggots. However, the person who trusts in the Living God – and follows His instructions by faith – will see provision at all times.

Waiting to Catch Up
(A Letter to the Apostle Paul)

We know that the whole creation has been groaning as in the pains of childbirth right up to the present time. Not only so, but we ourselves, who have the firstfruits of the Spirit, groan inwardly as we wait eagerly for our adoption as sons, the redemption of our bodies. For in this hope we were saved. But hope that is seen is no hope at all. Who hopes for what he already has? But if we hope for what we do not yet have, we wait for it patiently.

Romans 8:22-25 (NIV)

Thank you, Paul, for acknowledging that the best of us groan.

Ours is not a shallow whining or complaining; but a deep, aching sorrow for the brokenness we face.

You have gently reminded us that the entire earth cries out for redemption – to be bought back – to be restored – to be held in the hands of Jesus once and for all.

I remember, Paul, when you said we are pressed but not crushed.

In this jar of clay I call my body lives God Almighty.

When that pressing of life seems to be too strong for the walls I have sought to build around me, may I remember that the burden will not break me; for who can crush the infinite?

It is impossible that the pressure be too great for Jesus.

You said, Paul, we would be perplexed but never in despair.

I am perplexed. I am confused by many things.

By unanswered prayers – the ones that seem so right.

By the aching hearts of children in their innocence neglected.

By the aching hearts of adults in their willfulness alienated.

By injustice – seeing some have and some have not.

By loneliness never wished for, never intended.

By broken bodies.

By daily battles with disease.

By the last and greatest enemy of the living – death.

By all these things, my dear friend, Paul, I am perplexed.

But I am not in despair.

There is one thing of which I am sure . . . God makes sense of confusion.

Confusion is . . . seeing the Son of God lie in the feeding trough of animals.

Confusion is . . . seeing the Light of the universe being rejected by the darkness of men.

Confusion is . . . seeing the Lord of all creation crushed on a cross.

Confusion is . . . seeing a rock roll over the tomb of the Author of life.

Does God make sense of confusion?

Did the Son of God, Light of the universe, Lord of all, and Author of life stay in the trough, in the darkness, on the cross, or in the tomb?

No! God took the confusion, balled it up in His hands, breathed mercy upon it, and threw it back to us as droplets of hope.

And wherever the droplets of hope find a home, God comes to live.

Does God make sense of confusion?

Will unanswered prayers be left misunderstood?

Will aching hearts always writhe in pain?

Will lonely people never share laughter?

Will broken bodies never be fixed?

Will death always be the final pain we face?

No. No. No. A thousand times over . . . no.

Paul, you said we groan. You said we cry inside waiting for redemption.

As sure as the sun rises, that day will come.

As your friend, Peter, said, this is our "living hope."

Dipped inside my spirit is a droplet of hope from God's own hand.

This hope tells me it will all make sense someday.

This hope tells me we will be reunited in the end.

This hope tells me that as Jesus really came out of the tomb, we really will, too.

This old, broken body so ready to sin will one day fly heavenward.

I groan now. That is the reality of a broken person and a broken world.

But I will not groan forever.

God has redeemed my spirit, Paul. My emotions and my body are just waiting to catch up.

The Only Thing We Ever Really Have

"The earth is the LORD's, and everything in it; the world, and all who live in it."
Psalm 24:1 (NIV)

All the money in the world. Fame beyond imagination. A body to be envied. Success of unbelievable proportions. All of this is meaningless the moment we take our last breath. And, perhaps, all of this is meaningless right now. The world is filled with people who are scared on the inside because life on the outside does not provide security whatsoever.

Think about this: we cannot even guarantee we will have a heartbeat in the next five minutes. When we strip away all the pride and self-sufficiency, we realize we are helpless creatures – completely unable to secure our destinies. What do we ever really have?

All we ever really have is the opportunity to connect with our Creator. We are at His mercy; and His mercy provides the opportunity to reach out to Him and react to His desire to hold us tightly.

I cannot control the world. (That is quite an understatement!) I cannot control tomorrow. I cannot control people. I cannot control the continuance or discontinuance of my very earthly life. The Word of God makes clear that God alone owns everything and controls everything. In Psalm 24:1 (NIV), David penned, "The earth is the LORD's, and everything in it, the world, and all who live in it."

We may rebel against God's ultimate ownership and control, but the truth remains unchanged no matter our disagreement. Many people's ongoing denial of the sovereignty of God keeps them up at night, causes them internal and external distress, diseases their minds with discomfort and confusion, and saps them of the energy to live.

When a person comes to terms with the simple truth that the only thing he or she has is the opportunity for relationship with God, then a person is on the road to a life worth living. David also said in Psalm 111:10 that "the fear of the LORD is the beginning of wisdom." In other words, to stand in reverent awe of God – to recognize we are at His mercy – is the ultimate starting point for the wisdom necessary to navigate this world.

What is the way to the only *real* life there is? Admit that you are helpless in the shadow of the living Lord who created you. Ask Him to make things right between you and Him by the sacrifice of Himself – the death and resurrection of Jesus Christ, the second Person of the Godhead. In this sincere plea, we ask God to cover with the righteousness of Jesus our sin and inability to please Him.

What then? We *rest*. Isaiah proclaims in Isaiah 30:15 (NIV), "In repentance and rest is your salvation." We rest because we now finally and clearly see that the only thing we ever really have is the opportunity to connect with our Creator. Believing we are in control is a delusion, and one can never really rest in a lie. "Then you will know the truth, and the truth will set you free" (John 8:32, NIV).

What's Faster than the Speed of Light?

The royal official said to Him, "Sir, come down before my child dies." Jesus said to him, "Go; your son lives."

John 4:49-50a

Traveling at over eleven million miles per minute, light can circle the earth 7.5 times in one second! Able to cover nearly six trillion miles in a year, light surely moves at a rate of speed that staggers the mind. So what is it in this world that is faster than the speed of light? The mercy of God rushing toward the heart that desperately believes. The miracle of Jesus zooming toward sincere and yielded brokenness.

Can you see it now? In your mind's eye, can you picture the flashing glory of God's hand setting into motion His lightning-fast mercy on its way to the point of your need? The One who spoke all the molecular structures of the universe into being with an instantaneous word; He is the One that now speaks forth His answers for our desperate lives.

The royal official of John chapter four had access to some of the money, power, and dignity the world could offer. He also had a son who was dying. A stark realization no doubt flooded his soul, "I cannot persuade death with my power, I cannot buy life with my money, and my dignity is not enough to shut the jaws of darkness." Have we – like the royal official – ever been *there*? You know, in a place where we finally get it, where we finally comprehend our severe limitations.

The royal official travels some fifteen miles to get to Jeus to tell the Messiah that his son is at the point of death. No doubt having exhausted all medical possibilities and worldly privileges, the desperate man looks to the Savior. Though Jesus chastises the official at the outset for the status of his heart, the man of worldly nobility graciously accepts the rebuke of Jesus and presses forward respectfully with his need, "Jesus – Sir – please come to my town before my child dies."

Jesus then spoke those words we long to hear, those words of life. At the very instant our Savior tells the official his son will live, the miracle falls all over the boy. The fifteen miles between Jesus and the dying child become a literal nonentity. Smashed to oblivion is the span between the point of need and the Savior of the needy.

Desperation of a broken heart. *Realization* of the need for Jesus. *Activation* of something even faster than the speed of light: the movement of God, the Maker of light, toward a heart that yields and hopes in Him.

Cure for the Common Christmas Verse

She will bear a Son; and you shall call His name Jesus, for He will save His people from their sins.

Matthew 1:21

Oh, the careless treatment we often give the common "Christmas verse," Matthew 1:21. Regularly presented to us in the month of December, the powerful words are frequently taken for granted, "She will bear a Son; and you shall call His name Jesus, for He will save His people from their sins."

Since these are the words of the angel of the Lord to Joseph concerning the Son of God and His amazing placement by the Holy Spirit in the womb of Mary, we rightly consider these words momentous. Here stands the announcement that our infinite God has chosen to put on human flesh! And why? The angel proclaims plainly the motivation right at the inauguration of this unbelievable, sacrificial season of God's plan. The reason is so that we can be saved from our *sins*.

Notice God did not say, "He will save His people from their low self-esteem" or "from their lack of purpose" or "from their depressive hopelessness" or "from their illness" or "from their loneliness" or "from their economic hardship." No, God sounds forth the real answer for the human dilemma – salvation from sin.

All other difficulties are secondary to the root cause, which is sinfulness. Please cease looking primarily for Jesus to build your self-esteem or give you purpose or make you hopeful or heal your body or grant relationships or make you wealthy. Please, please, please . . . run to Jesus for the very reason He entered the bloody womb of a woman and grew to shed His own blood and sacrifice His life – to deliver you from sin.

At its putrid core, sin is selfishness. When I trust Jesus to deliver me from my self-centered plans and desires, I realize I now want what He wants. All other circumstances aside, I can now truly live, because my sin had been killing me.

Here is the clincher. He did not come to save us *despite* our sins, but *from* our sins. The Greek root is clear; Jesus came to separate us from our sin nature. He destroys that wicked union. The moment I run to Him, He obliterates the damning attachment of sin to my soul. His ultimate aim in the new world He prepares is to place an infinite distance of space and time between us and all sin's destructive and debilitating effects.

Are we currently living to be free from sin? Are we as hard-nosed about the mission as Jesus is? I think we suffer so much discontent not because of dismal situations, but because separation from sin – the goal of God – is not our goal. The most humane thing in the entire world is for a person created by God to have his or her union with sinfulness obliterated. Fear not other maladies, save this: a clinging to sin. Live for that for which our Savior lives: detachment from sin and attachment to God. All other solutions naturally follow – whether today, tomorrow, or in the place Jesus is preparing.

What determination Jesus had to exit glory and enter this broken world to save us from our sins! What determination will we have to refuse to gossip, to sacrifice that hour of time, to give that hard-earned money, to smile at that one who hurt us, to choose not to retaliate, to enter a sweet hour of prayer, to turn off the iPod and open up the Bible, to purposefully make Jesus the topic of dinner conversation, to put ourselves on the backburner tomorrow afternoon, to confess wrongdoing and ask forgiveness of a friend, or to distance ourselves from sin an any number of ways?

"Jesus came to save us from our sins," said the angel of the Lord.

How Will We Rest?

How precious to me are your thoughts, O God! How vast is the sum of them!
Psalm 139:17 (NIV)

How will we rest?
These racing thoughts do so entangle.

How will we rest?
These racing hearts do so encumber.

How will we rest?
Counseled to work it out, think it through, and make it happen.

How will we rest?
Striving hopelessly to look from every angle.
Striving nervously to prevail o'er every detail.

How will we rest?
Foolish, frail humanity.
Exasperated, tired humanity.
Our vanity stifles rest.

How will we rest?
We will look up.

We will see the glorious, downward flow of God's innumerable
and precious thoughts toward us.

We will stand at the base of the waterfall.

We will be washed in the reality of his immeasurably deep plans
for us as they pour over our racing minds and racing hearts.

We will be covered with the infinite purposes of our infinite
God.

How will we rest?
Not in our own striving.
Not in our own doing.
Not even in our own planning.

We will rest in the thoughts of God toward us.

Concerning God's "Harsh" Judgment of Sin

"Give thanks to the LORD, for he is good.
His love endures forever.
Give thanks to the God of gods.
His love endures forever.
. . . to him who alone does great wonders,
His love endures forever.
. . . who by his understanding made the heavens,
His love endures forever.
. . . to him who struck down the firstborn of Egypt
His love endures forever.
. . . who struck down great kings,
His love endures forever.
and killed mighty kings –
His love endures forever."
Psalm 136:1,2,4,5,10,17-18 (NIV)

"So Joshua subdued the whole region, including the hill country, the Negev, the western foothills and the mountain slopes, together with all their kings. He left no survivors. He totally destroyed all who breathed, just as the LORD, the God of Israel, had commanded."
Joshua 10:40 (NIV)

How do we explain difficult Scriptures as those above? God's love endures forever. He is good and does great wonders. That part is easy to swallow. But how do we reconcile His enduring love with striking down firstborn children and killing mighty kings? How do we understand God as He commanded Joshua to destroy every living thing in an entire region? We must take note of the following sentence and then observe its explanation:

It is *because* God's love endures forever that He must kill what would kill us.

Each soul makes a choice. If we choose God, we come under His protection. Our greatest battle becomes the battle against sin and its awful consequences and certain destruction. When God's chosen people entered the Promised Land, the heathen nations already occupying the land had chosen not to serve the Lord. Sin ruled them. If God had allowed them to remain, their sinful ways would eventually become a part of the Israelites' lives. Then the Israelites, too, would be destroyed by sin. God protects those who choose Him. Why would He allow both the unredeemed and the redeemed to be destroyed by sin's results? Instead, He urged His people to destroy all evil influence in order to establish a culture that leads to life and righteousness.

Today, in the age of grace, God does not ask us to destroy unredeemed people. Rather, we are to love them and try to bring them to Christ. However, we are to destroy and rid ourselves of all the sinful things that would destroy our spiritual lives. We must completely rid ourselves of sinful habits and influences in order to save our purity of spirit. *Sin always leads to death.*

The following illustration makes the point well that we must destroy sin in order to truly live:

As she lay there suddenly unconscious, he hovered over her body with his glistening knife. His accomplices nervously awaited his every move as beads of sweat dripped from his forehead despite the well-thought-out plan. He lifted his arm slightly . . . and then . . . it happened. His gloved hand began its descent toward her chest. The intense breathing could be heard from behind his mask. Then, swiftly, the glistening knife pierced her skin and went deeper, deeper. Within minutes the surgeon had removed the deadly bullet which had been lodged perilously close to her heart. She would recover.

This story seems horrifying at first. We become angry with this monstrous man who seems to be committing murder. However, by the end of the story, we understand that the doctor truly cares for the patient and is cutting her chest in order to save her life. We must not be angry with God for what He seeks to remove from our lives as He purifies us. He is really caring for us. May we let Him remove the "bullets of sin!"

Don't Fear Mixed Reactions

There was much grumbling among the crowds concerning Him; some were
saying, "He is a good man"; others were saying, "No, on
the contrary, He leads the people astray."

John 7:12

Don't fear mixed reactions as long as your character is not mixed-up!

Let me ask you a few questions before we go any further: Is Jesus perfect? Did Jesus ever lie? Hopefully, your answers are "yes" and then "no." Jesus is God, and so He is perfect and cannot lie. Even so, check out the following passages of Scripture (taken from John 4:39-40; 5:16, 18; 6:15; 7:12, and 7:43-44, respectively):

- "From that city many of the Samaritans **believed in Him** . . . they were asking Him to stay with them. . ."
- "For this reason the Jews were **persecuting Jesus**, . . ."
- "For this reason therefore the Jews were **seeking all the more to kill Him**, . . ."
- "So Jesus, perceiving that they were intending to come and take Him by force **to make Him king**, . . ."
- "There was much grumbling among the crowds concerning Him; **some were saying, 'He is a good man'**; others were saying, 'No, **on the contrary, He leads the people astray.'**"
- So a **division occurred in the crowd because of Him**.

Astonishingly, people had very mixed reactions to Jesus. Though Jesus is perfect and unchanging in unblemished character; we have some believing, some persecuting, some seeking to kill, and some wanting to make Him king. Generally, people were divided and displayed a wide array of emotions when it came to Jesus.

The variance of reaction is amazing, because the Person to whom everyone was reacting never varies. What do we learn from this? Even when we are acting within the will of God and reflecting His unchanging character, people may very well have mixed reactions to us! As human beings, our sole responsibility is to live abandoned to the will of God. As we remain unswervingly accountable to Him, let the chips fall where they may. Every person has individual reasons for reacting to God and others in the way that he does, and those reasons are dependent on the status of his own heart. We cannot control how people will respond.

If Jesus Christ – the impeccable Son of God – encountered mixed reactions, what should we expect? The thing on which we ought to focus is our own character. If people react badly to us because of our own wavering character, it is our fault. However, if people react badly to us because of the reflection of God's character within us, we must leave the consequences in the hands of God.

Bad Trees and End Results

A good tree cannot produce bad fruit, nor can a bad tree produce good fruit.
Every tree that does not bear good fruit is cut down and thrown into the fire.
Matthew 7:18-19

No matter what we say in the name of Jesus or do in the name of Jesus, God discerns the truth of the matter. It is quite possible for someone to prophesy in God's name and perform miracles without truly being a man or woman of God. Satan has the power to do counterfeit signs and wonders (II Thessalonians 2:9), and that will be one hallmark of the antichrist in the end times.

Jesus made clear to His disciples that they should examine fruit. In other words, we are to observe the end results of the life and work of a person. If my life does not please God, then neither does my purported work for Him. Though it is popular today to have a ministry for the Lord, this means nothing if we do not have a day-to-day way of living that pleases the Lord.

Jesus appeals to basic logic when He reminds us that it is simply impossible for a diseased tree to bring forth healthy fruit. If we are still diseased by sin at our core, our work for God will not heal the disease. The ultimate results of our lives will still wreak havoc.

I may appear to do great things for God, but if people walk away from interaction with me disturbed by my spitefulness and rattled by my lack of self-control, then I am not bearing the fruit of the Spirit of God. If the end results of my relationships are destruction and unrest, if I never follow-through in faithfulness, if selfish impatience is my prominent trait, if sadness and gloom surround me always, or if imperviousness marks my every path; I am bearing fruit that is diseased (See Galatians 5:22-23). The core of me needs fixed. For, "A good tree cannot produce bad fruit, nor can a bad tree produce good fruit" (Matthew 7:18).

To be sure we understand the seriousness of bad fruit, Jesus said, "Many will say to Me on that day, 'Lord, Lord, did we not prophesy in Your name, and in Your name cast out demons, and in Your name perform many miracles?' And then I will declare to them, 'I never knew you; DEPART FROM ME, YOU WHO PRACTICE LAWLESSNESS'" (Matthew 7:22-23). You see, in Heaven it will not be necessary for people to cast out demons, prophesy, or perform miracles. What will be essential is the love between brethren and all the kindness, gentleness, and self-control that comes with real love.

A grave issue stands at hand. Let us grapple with it. Diseased trees bear diseased fruit. Alleged work for the Lord notwithstanding, "Every tree that does not bear good fruit is cut down and thrown into the fire" (Matthew 7:19). It is the truth of our lives that matters, not what we appear to be because of all kinds of ministry efforts. This is a matter of integrity; what are we at the root? Because what we are will come out in the everyday effects of our living.

Why would Jesus throw a diseased tree into the fire? Good fruit will never come from it. The eternity the people of God want to enter is a forever of good things. The eternity fitting of our holy God is a forever of righteousness. What is – at its core – not good, must go.

Before the time of Jesus' teaching what we have briefly discussed, He preached clearly, "Repent, for the kingdom of heaven is at hand" (Matthew 4:17). If your soul is diseased and you recognize it, there is hope for you. Jesus proclaims, "Repent." Turn around. Change your mind completely. Recognize that the core needs healed. Realize more work will not change you. Decide that you need Jesus to clean your heart. He will. He promises that the kingdom of heaven – of goodness – is right around the corner.

He Will Get Us There!

> So they were willing to receive Him into the boat, and immediately the boat
> was at the land to which they were going.
>
> John 6:21

Do you wonder how you'll get to where you need to go? Do you doubt that you'll make it to the destination God has for you? If you're thinking destination with a capital "D" – Heaven – let's add to that the myriad of smaller harbors along the way as we traverse this life. How will we make it?

We must embrace the exciting truth of one of the most over-looked, under-appreciated verses in the Bible, John 6:21. Here, John relates to us the power of Jesus to manipulate the very fabric of space and time for the safe transportation of His followers to their destination! Unbelievable, science fiction-like action is displayed here. But this is not fiction. This is the Maker of reality manipulating reality under the feet of His followers!

After Jesus walked on water to get to His disciples' boat out on that old sea, our Savior was finally invited into the vessel. He had to convince His friends that He was not a ghost, as His supernatural power overwhelmed them.

Although Matthew and Mark focus more on the water-walking in their Gospels, John zooms in precisely on the next miracle: "So they were willing to receive Him into the boat, and immediately the boat was at the land to which they were going" (John 6:21).

Astounding! That boat was transported supernaturally to the shore. Overpowering space and time, Jesus carried the vessel of His feeble-minded followers! In an instant – without added effort and rowing – there they were, at the other side.

Why did Jesus manipulate the fabric of the created universe that day? Of the infinite number of reasons God may have, we can be sure one is for our current comfort. We need tangible examples of God's control of circumstances on our behalf. Who knows how Jesus will transport us to tomorrow, or past this difficult trial, or over this heart-wrenching disappointment, or to the future years of our life, or through the tumultuous times of our culture, or over the anxiety that would destroy us? But He can. And He will . . . if we let Him into our boat.

Of Fountains and Vacuums

For my people have committed two evils: they have forsaken Me, the fountain
of living waters, to hew for themselves cisterns, broken
cisterns that can hold no water.
Jeremiah 2:13

When we turn away from God, we are not simply turning to something "not quite as good" as God; we are veering toward a veritable vacuum. When we choose to disregard God, we actually descend into a vortex that sucks the vitality of life from the core of us. Our Creator spoke through the prophet Jeremiah, "For my people have committed two evils: they have forsaken Me, the fountain of living waters, to hew for themselves cisterns, broken cisterns that can hold no water" (Jeremiah 2:13).

Evil number one: people turn from God, who is – metaphorically – the Fountain (or Spring) of Living Water. As earthly springs provide a fresh flow of natural water, so God is the source of real life and joy. Spring water is not produced through our efforts, but rather enjoyed when we come near and drink. The supply is endless; it just keeps coming, and we drink happily though we've not had one bit to do with the water's production. The refreshment is ours; the production is His. What utter shame it is that we would walk away from the source of all life and joy. It is more than a shame; it is sheer evil to forsake the One who provides.

Evil number two: people turn to man-made cisterns – broken cisterns – that can hold no water. Make no mistake; when we abandon the Fountain of Life, there is no hope of gathering life in containers of our making. Whatever containers we fashion to feebly attempt to hold joy – riches, successes, relationships, fit bodies, etc. – they simply cannot hold life. As with broken cisterns leaking water, real joy leaks out of these containers – sometimes oozing, sometimes gushing.

Living for God and living for something else are not opposites. Living for something other than God is the absence of genuine life. As broken containers leak water, so people turned away from God leak the essence of life. God is the Fountain, the Giver of all good things. All else is a broken cistern, sucking true vitality from our soul.

What is evil? To turn from the Source of Life and turn to a vacuum, thinking we have somehow done better for ourselves. Come back to God.

The Scent of Autumn

While the earth remains, seedtime and harvest, and cold and heat, and summer and winter, and day and night shall not cease.

Genesis 8:22

Sitting in my backyard on a gorgeous autumn afternoon, I reached down and picked up a handful of leaves from the ground. As the brown and yellow leaves crackled in my hands, I remembered days of my childhood. I would rake a pile of autumn leaves and carve out a hole in the center. I would then sit there, delightfully surrounded by the leaves, as I read book after book. Days seemed simple then, and my memory of reading in the leaves is amazingly vivid. As I lay in the pile of leaves consuming my books, my heart would leap as my imagination ran wild with all the possibilities of life.

Now a grown adult, I was tempted to smell the crackling autumn leaves in my hand. Knowing that our sense of smell is greatly related to memory, I took time to hold those leaves close to my face and breathe deeply. Ah . . . the comfort of childhood days came rushing back.

What amazed me was the constancy of the smell of the autumn leaves. Though my childhood reading in the fallen leaves occurred decades earlier, the scent of those leaves is exactly the same. I know not much of the biology and chemistry behind dying leaves, but I know this: they smell the same today as they did then.

Much else has changed in the decades between my experiences, but the scent of autumn is constant. God promised in Genesis 8:22, "While the earth remains, seedtime and harvest, and cold and heat, and summer and winter, and day and night shall not cease." The changing of seasons and all the accompanying details continue on unhindered *because God is a God of constancy*. He is a Savior on whom we can fully rely. The God who said, "Let the earth bring forth vegetation, plants, and trees" is a God we can trust. His way of cycling the leaves through life and death – and all the reactions producing the smell of autumn – will continue on as long as the earth endures.

And when earth no longer does endure – when this broken planet has to flee from the presence of a righteous God (Revelation 20:11) – our Savior will still be reliable. He is the one constant in all of life. He will re-make this earth into a home of righteousness for the redeemed.

As the earth and its current regularity remind us of God's constancy, so the return of Jesus and His re-making of this old earth remind us that only God is unchanging. Though the scent of autumn goes on and on in this life, the God who created autumn will outlast this world. He alone is the One on whom we can depend to usher in the next world, and carry us there.

The Mercy Seat of an Infinite God

Thus says the LORD, "Heaven is My throne, and earth is My footstool."
Isaiah 66:1a (NKJV)

Listen to what God says, for what man says is of no consequence unless it aligns with the Almighty's revelation. Quite vital to remember is that God has spoken, and His Word is distinct and above all else (Psalm 138:2). Set God's Word at the forefront, or risk succumbing to the relentless temptation to believe the prevalent, mundane thought that God is small and weak and not altogether different from us. "Thus says the LORD" is a phrase meant to shake our paradigm, as we are so apt to focus on anything or anyone other than the Creator from whom all things derive.

God cannot be contained, nor can He be measured; incalculable is His nature (I Kings 8:27). Yet in daily thoughts and actions, we reason that we understand how God has worked, or is working, or will work in various situations of life. With Heaven as His throne and Earth as His footstool, God's infinite nature staggers the imagination. The visible heavens, the innumerable parts of the universe we are still completely unable to access, and the very abode of God – all of these exist as His throne. God is infinitely greater than all the heavens, able to encapsulate and harness each part for His purposes. Our Creator is the one who "works all things according to the counsel of His will" (Ephesians 1:11b). His unfathomable power unceasingly pulls all aspects of life – physical, emotional, and spiritual – toward His ultimate will. The Maker of all that exists will irrefutably have the final word over all that exists!

Stunning is the truth that earth is God's footstool. We humans have not yet explored all the depths of any particular ocean, we have barely begun the first leg of the journey into any miniscule portion of the vastness of space, and we have not yet plunged into all the depths of the mystery of the molecular; still God refers to the earth as His footstool. He means for us to know that His magnificence cannot be calculated. Metaphorically, that upon which He rests His feet is immensely more than that with which we can even commence to grapple. Therefore, it would be ridiculous for us to grow hopeless concerning circumstances of the earth, for God says of this place, "That is simply my footstool."

How would it be to know that the God who created everything from nothing and rightfully boasts Heaven as His throne is willing to be with us? To talk with us? To hear our heart and stay with us? To carry our burdens? To share His presence in real relationship? We can know this joy because the specific footstool of God in the Old Testament is the Ark of the Covenant (I Chronicles 28:2) Our Creator desires to rest with us – to "put His feet up" if you will – that we may have a genuine relationship with Him.

This relationship seems impossible, though, given the eternal nature of God, His unfathomable power, and His holiness. This seeming impossibility steps back and disappears into the shadow of the Ark of the Covenant and its treasured mercy seat. The mercy seat marked the separation between the Law and God's manifest presence. In the ark, below the mercy seat – or atonement cover – rested the tablets of the Law. Above the mercy seat – between the gold cherubim – God's glorious presence came. Although every person ever born on earth ultimately longs to be in God's presence where all is right and joyous, most try to imagine the longings and emptiness of life could be satisfied in some other manner. Hence, Isaiah 53:6 (NIV) proclaims, "Each of us has turned to his own way." Still, the only way to right and hope and peace and ultimate, coveted fulfillment is to be in God's presence – to rest with Him.

We ask, "How will I get to God, for I am constantly dragged down by this law below?" Each time we attempt to rise up and rest with our Creator between those cherubim, the tablets full of commandments we cannot keep pull us back down beneath the atonement cover. We feel as Paul did in Romans chapter seven asking how he could possibly be delivered from his failure to do what he knows to be right. Do we also feel the victory Paul knew as communicated in Romans 8:3 (NKJV), "For what the law could not do in that it was weak through the flesh, God did by sending His own Son in the likeness of sinful flesh"? God forbid we ever forget the mercy seat lies between the law and God's presence as a clear delineation of our hope. For, on that mercy seat, the blood of the sacrifice was applied. Symbolically – via the animal sacrifice – the blood of Jesus was sprinkled on that cover to settle the matter and forever absorb our inability to fulfill God's law. Through the blood of Jesus, we can rise above hopelessness and enter God's safety despite our own sinfulness. Quite literally, we rise from being pitiful creatures condemned by the law to being God's own children, with access to His blessed presence. How does this happen? The blood of Jesus on the mercy seat opens up the way and we rise to God through the blood of His own Son.

The thought of Jesus' blood opening up the way for sinful man to gain relationship with a holy God breeds yet another thought: there is nothing stronger than the blood of Jesus. No sin, no failure, no amount of inadequacy can stop Jesus from giving to us access to God. That mercy seat of the Old Testament was made of pure gold. Metaphorically speaking, our spirits rise from the lower compartment of the condemnation of the law to the upper space of freedom and joy, ever watched by the cherubim that long to know this miracle of salvation. How do we rise since the atonement cover of pure gold lies between the law and God's presence? We can rise because the apostle tells us in I Peter 1:18-19 (NKJV) that we are "not redeemed with corruptible things like silver or gold ...but with the precious blood of Christ..." Gold, though highly treasured and often tried by fire, is yet corruptible – a substance that ultimately succumbs to disintegration. Not so the blood of Jesus! It is precious, incorruptible, just like our heavenly inheritance. That timeless, infinitely powerful blood blasts through any obstacle that hinders us from reaching God!

God, who is infinite and has spoken all things into existence with just His breath, can accurately say that this realm – this terrain – on which we live out our limited days, is so small and powerless compared to Him that He boasts it as the place to rest His feet. This same God is sure to remind us that of all the locations on this planet, the place on which He focused for His resting is the Ark of the Covenant. Why? Because the personal rest and relationship all humanity needs with the God who created us can only be found where the blood is applied and opens up the way for sinful people to commune with holy God. The funnel representing God's rest and communion with us narrows down to one point – the place where the blood is applied.

The Best

For it is God who is at work in you, both to will and to work for
His good pleasure.

Philippians 2:13

Will I do the right thing?
Will I want the right thing?
Will I accomplish that thing in the end?

All the "wills" shall be answered
One way, one day –

In the way that recalls the Giver of right,
In the day that pins all hope on Him.

God energizes my will to want right.
God energizes my flesh to do right.
God brings about what pleases Him.

God is at work in me.

He makes me want the best, and
He enables me to live the best,

When I realize the **best** is **His pleasure**.

When God Calls

The Lord will fulfill his purpose for me; your love, O Lord, endures forever – do not abandon the works of your hands.

Psalm 138:8 (NIV)

When God calls you to love,
Love to the end,
Because God never fails.

When God calls you to hope,
Hope despite looming impossibility,
Because God can do all things.

When God calls you to be a fool for His sake,
Be a fool despite the press of pride,
Because God came to earth in all humility.

When God calls you to give,
Give without fear of loss,
Because God is of infinite resource.

When God calls you to persevere against all odds,
Persevere despite exhaustion,
Because God gives strength to the weary.

When God calls you to live for Him,
Live for Him though it sometimes appears not to matter,
Because God fulfills every purpose under Heaven for His own.

A Stirring Compliment

Let us hold fast the confession of our hope without wavering, for He
who promised is faithful.

Hebrews 10:23

Recently I received a compliment that moved me deeply. I had the honor of speaking to Christian school teachers and administrators at a convention in Washington, D.C., given by the Association of Christian Schools International (ACSI). I presented a seminar about a Biblical approach to classroom management. The seminar was presented over a period of two days, during four sessions, spanning a total of five and one-half hours; and my accompanying PowerPoint presentation contained ninety-two slides.

The fact that a seminar on classroom management can be so filled with moments of inspiration by God's Holy Spirit is a topic for another day. Let me just say that the attendees' hearts were ready to receive God's Word; and *any* topic of discussion can and should be driven toward its Creator. Classroom management becomes a lively subject when viewed through the lens of God's Word. Jesus is the Master Teacher and the Maker of all students. Learning is His wonderful idea in the first place, and He has something to say about it being done effectively and joyfully!

Now we go back to the pivotal input I was blessed to receive. The last half-hour of the final session was going very well, when I realized I had twenty-five minutes to finish presenting the material so that we could all culminate our study with prayer. Part of the last session involved me darting to various parts of the ballroom in which I was presenting, as I demonstrated the importance of spending time in each quadrant of a classroom and the vital nature of a "change in scenery" for students in order to keep everyone just a little off balance for an active learning environment. This final stretch of the seminar was definitely as active as the first few moments had been the day before. My energy level was high, and the audience was engaged.

Things were going so well that we hardly noticed a few other seminars had already ended – ended early I might mention. The last session was to finish at 3:00 pm. However, some attendees of other seminars began heading to the lobby of the hotel as early as 2:40 pm. As a presenter, my intent was to provide instruction until the very end. The delegates had paid money to attend the convention, and many were receiving continuing education credit for the instructional hours of my seminar.

Finally, I began the closing prayer, which – apparently – was put forth with much passion. For, no sooner had I said, "Amen," than the regional associate director for ACSI approached me right before he quickly began to disassemble the equipment as he prepared for his own departure. As someone who has known and worked with me for quite a few years, his words went something like this: "Well, Shelli, I would have expected no less from you! You kept teaching right up to the end . . . and with such vigor. Even the closing prayer was so 'right on.' Thank you for being faithful."

No one could have wiped the smile from my face in that moment. Even as people in the hallways scurried off, some of my students lingered to talk and ponder God's work together. And I had received an invaluable commendation; I had been faithful, reflecting the heart of God.

Paul tells us in Hebrews 10:23, "Let us hold fast the confession of our hope without wavering, for He who promised is faithful." Yes, we can depend upon our God; He is faithful! Moreover, the reason we humans can hold onto the Christian faith without wavering is precisely because the One who makes His promise to us is faithful. It is not because of me that I can persevere; it is because of the One who promised His goodness to me. When the apostle admonishes us to keep going in our faith – to endure – to persist – he is sure to tell us *why* we can do so: *He who promised* is faithful.

God finishes what He starts. God always keeps His Word. God does not grow weary and desert the cause. God does not wear down when things get difficult. God does not lose interest. God is faithful to the end. Hebrews 12:2 tells us that He is both the Author and the Finisher of our faith. Philippians 1:6 says that He who began a good work in us will complete it. With our Lord, we "get our money's worth"! He does not stick with us only half-heartedly; He stays with us completely and vigorously.

When I think about the analogy to my classroom management seminar, I think of it this way. The last ten minutes of my last session were as strong as the first ten minutes of my first session. The content and passion remained unchanged. And so it is with life. During the last few moments of our earthly life, God will be as true to us as He was when He formed us in the womb. Amazingly, though, His faithfulness extends to the next world. Forever and ever He will remain our strength – even in the glory of Heaven. Though my seminar had an ending point, the goodness of God has no limit; it continues into the next life without end. Remember Psalm 36:5? "Your lovingkindness, O LORD, extends to the heavens, Yourfaithfulnessreaches to the skies."

Thank you, Dr. Hegedus, for a compliment that stirs my heart. When we are faithful to the end, we reflect the heart of our Savior. I pray today that you and I will be faithful to the end in every endeavor – big or small – and even as we cross that chasm between this life and the next. We can if remember that "He who promised is faithful."

Fear of God Is Freeing

Better is a little with the fear of the LORD than great treasure and turmoil with it.
Proverbs 15:16

Fear of God is not a negative; it is the most positive thing in the cosmos. As a culture, we have largely lost the fitting view of the transcendent God. We have become all too familiar with Him, treating Him as if He existed for our pleasure. To the dismay of many, the facts stand quite the opposite. We exist for His pleasure. The reason I breathe is to bring glory to Him. This is in no way a restrictive concept, but one that catapults me into the mystery of unbounded hope.

When a person does not view God as the grandest and deserving of all dedication, that person will be in turmoil. Nothing aligns properly under the dominion of self. Why? Self is a false sovereignty, and operation on a false premise leads to a false conclusion. God is the only self-existent One. He made all things and all people. He has right of ownership. And the owned ones find their peace in His purpose. The designer knows how the design must operate in order to be what it was meant to be.

Proverbs 15:16 makes clear, "Better is a little with the fear of the Lord than great treasure and turmoil with it." Shattering the misconceptions of the self-absorbed, we come to terms with the fact that very little material gain in this world is far superior to much treasure accompanied by the unrest of minds that refuse to accept the sovereignty of God.

God must be revered for peace to flood into the human heart. God made me. I will answer to Him for the following: the life He gave me, the body He gave me, the moments He gave me, the heart He gave me, the mind He gave me, the influence He gave me, and every single breath He brings. He is to be feared because He demands an answer for my life. He demands payment for my sin.

He superintends my destiny and prescribes my eternity. I ought to be in awe of Him. He alone is holy.

When my heart properly fears this sovereign God, tumult flees my soul. For then, He is in His proper place – at the helm. My reverence for Him drives me to His saving grace, where Jesus stands as my righteousness. My awe of Him hastens me to love Him more and seek to understand whatever mysteries of Him He graces me to know. My respect for who He actually is compels me to yield my life to His cause.

Yes, I can live vibrantly with very little because fear of God is in my heart. The accumulation of earthly goods and distractions do not deliver what the human soul desperately needs. We do not need more; we need to rightly direct all we do have. We need to direct the entire realm of our lives to the One to Whom we owe everything. Whether I have little or much is no matter; the state of my heart in relation to God determines my level of peace.

Put off no longer the pursuit of God because He demands to be feared. Reverence for the sovereign God is the only way to live without distress. The reality is that He made you, and you will answer to Him. This should place you in a state of awe – not awe that leads to nervousness, but awe that leads to deliverance. We are free when we worship the One we ought to rightly revere. We were made for it.

Implications of Worry

> But seek first His kingdom and His righteousness, and all these
> things will be added to you.
>
> Matthew 6:33

Current brain research demonstrates that students under the distress of anxious thoughts do not learn as well as is possible. Stress and worry have a distinct negative impact on a person's ability to process and work properly with new information. In fact, Willis (2006) notes in regard to PET scans and fMRI scans,

> [These] reveal significant disturbances in the brain's learning circuits and chemical messengers when subjects are studied in stressful learning environments. In particular, the amygdala becomes overstimulated by stress, and in that hypermetabolic state, information cannot pass from sensory awareness into the memory connection and storage regions of the brain. (58)

Research is making clear that stress is a disruptor, causing a break in the normal processes of learning. If you will, it is as if the brain process becomes broken when anxiety appears on the scene. The emotional state rises to prominence, and deep and rational connections cannot be made. As Sprenger (2005) notes, "The brain is captivated by the emotion and turns attention to it. When these emotions capture the brain's attention, working memory is flooded and cannot be effective in working with the task at hand." (22) In fact, Willis (2006) posits,

> If the state of anxiety and stress is prolonged, it can lead to destruction and loss of critical connecting dendrites and synapses in the hippocampus. This means that new information does not reach the brain regions where it needs to be processed, associated with previous knowledge and experience, and stored for later recall. (60)

Obviously, then, heightened and prolonged anxiety inhibits true learning. Our bodies are designed for optimal learning when a general sense of peace and safety is present. My mind goes to Adam and Eve in the garden, as they were given the entire created world to explore and learn and work. While walking unhindered with their Creator, this process was a beautiful one. However, human rebellion against our God has brought disruption and misery to all the processes of life. This world is now broken; and so are we and all the functions of body and life. Fear floods in when a heart completely yielded to God goes out.

Jesus instructs His followers in Matthew 6:25, "Do not be worried about your life, as to what you will eat or what you will drink; nor for your body, as to what you will put on." The Greek word for worry in this quote comes from a root that means "to be drawn in different directions; to be divided, separated into parts, or cut in pieces." Wow; to be worried is essentially to have a divided mind! That is precisely what worrying feels like – our mind is cut in pieces so that we cannot stay focused on what matters. We are distracted and irritable and may even begin to feel hopeless. The mind was not meant to be divided, but whole.

Recall that brain research informs us of the dividing nature of anxiety. Students who are under stress simply cannot learn well because the entire process of learning becomes broken. Recall also Jesus' answer to worry in our lives: "But seek first [God's] kingdom and His righteousness, and all these things will be added to you" (Matthew 6:33). Jesus tells us here to not allow our minds to be divided by giving undue attention to the basic needs of life. The stress of worrying about these things slices our minds and hearts into distracted pieces; we are no longer able to do what ought to be done – focus on God.

Worry is sin because it goes against the will of God for us. We are designed by God to seek His kingdom and righteousness with all our heart. Jesus proclaims the cure for worry is to unite our mind under one goal: Him! In fact, God promises to add to our life all that we need for daily living as we commit to an undivided heart and mind. If we seek His kingdom first, then He will properly align the needs of life for us *underneath* the main goal. Picture first a troubled face with a myriad of worries stretching out all over in a scattered maze *above* his head; this is a worried person. Picture now a smiling face with all the needs of life being brought up to him in a straight line from *below* his head; this is a person who is trusting in God's promise.

As brain research tells us about classroom learning, so it goes with thinking for all of life. If my mind is to be used for God's glory – focused on His Word and His will – my mind needs to be united and peaceful. The division of worry destroys the purpose for which the mind was created – to grow in God's kingdom.

I submit to you another Biblical example of the truth concerning worry and learning. When Jesus spoke to His disciples about their future persecution, He boldly proclaimed in Luke 12:11-12,

When they bring you before the synagogues and the rulers and the authorities, do not worry about how or what you are to speak in your defense, or what you are to say; for the Holy Spirit will teach you in that very hour what you ought to say.

Jesus here tells us that our mind need not be divided because of the future. Jesus is instructing his disciples about a future event, and He wants them to be assured that He is already in the future. When the moment in time comes for the disciples to answer the authorities, God Himself (the Holy Spirit) will teach them what to say. Notice the use of the word *teach*. We can truly learn when our mind is focused on God and not divided by anxiety.

This Scripture passage is particularly amazing to me because of its clear implication: God connects our future needs with His present peace. Because our Lord is timeless, He is not bound to one moment or another. He is with us now, and He is in the future.

He has the authority to assure us that our minds need not be preoccupied with future concerns. When the need arises, the power of the Lord for that particular moment will come to light. His available power for our tomorrow is as sure as His available peace for our today.

Teachers of our day ought to heed the Bible first and foremost. In doing so, they will marvel at the alignment of true scientific discovery with God's Word. An atmosphere of peace and safety promotes better learning than an atmosphere of stress.

Moreover, people everywhere ought to heed God's command to live a life focused purely on Him. The root of the sin of worry in the Biblical sense is the idea of a mind divided. This division keeps me from serving God wholeheartedly. This division also causes the human brain to function at a reduced capacity; the learning process breaks. God wants us to learn and learn well. Learning of Him and the creation He has graciously given is a blessing we enjoy now, and we will enjoy it eternally in a home of righteousness, if Jesus is our Savior.

Enoch's Extraordinary Life

By faith Enoch was taken from this life, so that he did not experience death; he could not be found, because God had taken him away. For before he was taken, he was commended as one who pleased God.

Hebrews 11:5 (NIV)

Enoch lived an extraordinary life and escaped physical death as a result. Though this grand blessing is obviously not the norm in God's scheme of things, we certainly gain insight into the incredible things that can happen when we actually live a life pleasing to God.

The general description of eight of nine men in the genealogy of Genesis chapter five is that each one lived a certain number of years, fathered a certain son, lived a certain more number of years, had other children, and died. Enoch's description stands out as markedly different: instead of dying, he simply "was not," for God took him away. The exact details are not divulged, but this man did not have to die a physical death. Both Enoch's body and spirit were taken directly by God!

Genesis tells us that Enoch walked with God, and Hebrews 11:5 reveals in greater detail that Enoch pleased God. Enoch's walking with God was no doubt an intimate, passionate relationship. Certainly the man put God at the forefront and is now forever known for living above the ordinary and experiencing a miracle indeed.

The genealogy of Genesis chapter five makes clear that one man of many saw life as more than an accumulation of years and the building of a family. The span of each man's years represents a myriad of endeavors, including his work, his care for his family, his eating, his relaxation, his ponderings, etc. But, of all those things in which Enoch was also no doubt involved, none compared to Enoch's walk with God. His heart must have always been driven by a love for His Creator and Savior; his mind must have pushed all other activities to align with God's view.

For Enoch, this love for God was real. I Chronicles 28:9 informs us that God actively searches our hearts and understands every intention. Neither Enoch nor any one of us can get away with falsifying our passion. God knows our core. Enoch's right living was motivated by a desire to please God.

Following the effective description of Enoch in Hebrews 11:5, verse six goes on to tell us there are two requirements for drawing near to God; believing in His existence and believing that He rewards those who seek Him. Enoch staked his life on the existence of the one, true God who requires that we live for Him with all our heart, soul, and mind. Enoch was not disappointed.

One thing for which we ought to pray is such an unbroken walk with Jesus that our death is simply a seamless transition to the glorious continuance of eternal life. Though we will die physically (if Jesus does not return before then), our spirit will not miss a beat because of how close we are to our Lord.

God upholds Enoch as a shining example of God's power to do miraculous things for those who earnestly seek Him. If God translated a man to Heaven without death near the beginning of history, what is He trying to communicate to us in terms of our pursuits and expectations?

Jesus will completely destroy death, as outlined in I Corinthians 15:26. Death is the last enemy. Death is the result of man's sin against God. Death makes men fear. But Enoch looked forward to Jesus. He loved and believed in Him so much that Jesus gave Enoch a taste of the end at the beginning. May we allow God to so redeem us and pervade our lives that we, too, can taste His glory even as we walk this earth.

God may not translate us to Heaven without death, but Jesus promises us in John 5:24 that we have already passed from death to life when we hear Jesus and genuinely believe in Him. He gives us life and victory over sin and over ordinary, mundane circumstances. He then reveals that one day everyone whose body is in a tomb will hear His voice. Those who walked with Him in this life will have their body resurrected for eternal life, and those who walked without Him in this life will have their bodies resurrected for eternal judgment.

Pleasing God clearly means life eternal. For Enoch – and for us – it means amazing things are possible. The question is: how closely are we walking with God?

Inaccessibly High Over "Indestructible" Anxiety

The name of the Lord is a strong tower; the righteous run to it and are safe.
Proverbs 18:10 (NIV)

I begin with a quote of Robert J. Samuelson in a December 2010 issue of *Newsweek*: "From CEOs to ordinary families, we are a nation that is more cautious, more fearful, and more risk averse. This widespread and – so far – indestructible anxiety has hobbled the [economic] recovery. . ."

"Indestructible anxiety." Wow. Perhaps those words do not really need time to sink in to your mind, because the force behind them is already there. Our world is tumultuous and burdensome. The economy has gotten the best of many otherwise stable people and companies. The relentless pressure to do more and have more has catapulted otherwise content people to the brink of insanity. From anxiety over an unhealthy body type to concern for retirement years, people are restless; citizens are panicked.

May I remind Christians of their status? We are genuine citizens of another realm. The administration of our affairs currently takes place in a domain that is transcendent. Do not take lightly the truth of Philippians 4:20 (NIV), "But our citizenship is in heaven." Indeed, God superintends my life from the heavenly realm. Anxiety is *not* indestructible, for my Lord directs the moments of my life from the throne of His indisputable authority. No stock market crash, illness, unforeseen circumstance, or injustice can thwart the plan of the God who made the universe (Genesis 1:1), owns the world (Psalm 24:1), and drives all circumstances to serve His ultimate purpose (Ephesians 1:11).

Let us make this uncannily personal. Proverbs 18:10 (NIV) proclaims, "The name of the Lord is a strong tower; the righteous run to it and are safe." It is true that our culture gives us much about which to be concerned. Samuelson (2010) posits, "There is a wall of worry whose cause transcends the recession's severity. We now fear not only what we know but also what we don't." However, the Lord's own name – His glory – is a strong tower to which the Lord's children can run.

When we run, we are safe. The Hebrew term here used for "safe" means "inaccessibly high." In other words, we run to the Lord, and He lifts us up so that we stand insurmountably high above that which might destroy us! The tower of His glory is unavailable to the enemy. I picture in my mind all the worries of life reaching their icy fingers to snatch me, but they are unsuccessful because my life looms far above their grasp in the tower of God's glory.

The key is to run to that tower. When someone runs, they are making a bold statement to all observers. A runner makes clear the necessity of his destination. When seemingly indestructible anxiety moves in on me, I cannot hesitate. I need to sprint to God's tower without wavering. I cannot ponder other possibilities; there is no other safe place. Only God makes me inaccessibly high as He simultaneously and sovereignly rules both the universe and the intricate details of my life from His heavenly, transcendent throne.

God above is the Administrator of my affairs – not the national debt, the unemployment rate, the political landscape, the doctor's report, the rising incidence of depression, the unjust boss, or any other entity. We stand inaccessibly high over "indestructible" anxiety.

Stillness at the Windowpane

Be still and know that I am God . . .

Psalm 46:10 (NIV)

Human solitude and quietness are popular concepts in today's world, right? Wrong. Our culture is fast-paced, high-tech, and pseudo-connected. To speak of the grandeur of moments of human solitude and quietness is similar to speaking an alien language.

Our culture's general averseness to quiescence should be no surprise to the child of God who is well aware of the enemy's schemes. In this cosmic battle for the heart of man, Satan knows the power of preoccupation, restlessness, busyness, and noise. If we can be kept from outright meditation on the Lord and from serious introspection, the enemy will have his way in our lives.

"Be still and know that I am God." These beautiful words of Psalm 46:10 (NIV) invite us to perceive, to understand, and to learn that God is God! How? We gain this knowledge sometimes through being still. The Hebrew root for stillness tells us to cease from our own attempts and acknowledge the bigness and holiness of God.

Recently I stood nearly motionless at the window of my home office as a gentle, steady snow began. The huge evergreens lining the back of our property provided a wonderful, contrasting background for the gigantic "snow globe" type of snowflakes descending from the sky. I had been praying, and I felt the Lord prompt me to stay standing, arm leaning on the top of the lower windowpane. I know He wanted me to remain quiet and still, observing His creation and allowing Him to speak to me and calm my spirit. (So often we want to tell God things, but He also wants us to listen.)

I remained there purposefully for some time, watching glistening snowflakes. Actually, I tried following with my eyes a few individual flakes in their descent to the ground below. Against the dark green trees, the seemingly innumerable snowflakes amazed me. There was such an abundance of particles, but each one was traveling a unique path to join the others as they formed a white blanket on the grass. I found myself in the middle of Job 37:14-16 (NIV), "Stop and consider God's wonders. Do you know how God controls the clouds and makes his lightning flash? Do you know how the clouds hang poised, those wonders of him who is perfect in knowledge?"

Standing in the quiet of my home, leaning on the windowpane, watching snow fall, and obeying God's command to be still and consider Him; I was truly changed. I had been praying for days about many circumstances – some acutely troubling. As I stood at the window quietly knowing my Lord, He answered me without giving me exact answers. He filled my heart with courage. He renewed my strength and outlook as I allowed the noise of life to vanish in the stillness of moments given over to the Lord.

Amazingly, specific answers began to come in the days following. God directly reacted to my simple obedience with a cascade of answers, revelations, and peace. My flesh wants to work so hard for answers. Sometimes we want to drown out the hurt with a myriad of activities. We may even try to evade conviction of God's Holy Spirit with noise and preoccupation. Please do not give in to these tactics of the enemy. Treat with precious respect the godly concepts of quietness and human solitude. God works in these . . . as He promised.

Living and True

You turned to God from idols to serve a living and true God. . .
I Thessalonians 1:9b

The God of the Bible is both living and true. The apostle Paul here rejoices in the salvation of people from the first century city of Thessalonica, an influential place of commerce and philosophy. Paul magnifies a simple, yet life-altering, truth: his God is alive and his God is the "real deal."

I, as Paul, have staked my life on the God of the Bible. The fact that my God is living is of utmost importance to me. Because God is living, we need not fear the relentlessly successive moments of life. He is with me at this moment, and He will surely be with me in the next; for He is not static or feeble, but alive!

Because God is living, we can rest in the comfort of relationship with Him through Jesus. My God is not an object, or a conscious-ness, or a mere higher being; my God is a Person. When I call on Him by word or thought, He answers. I walk with a living God; I am not trying in vain to harness an impersonal power.

Because God is alive, I know the realities of my heart can be dealt with. For God's Word is also alive (Hebrews 4:12). He – by His Word and Spirit – can go to the deepest recesses of my heart and discern all that is there. Every motivation can be brought to light. God is holy and vibrant and willing to search me and convict me and forgive me and heal me. Every crack and crevice of my soul can be filled by the hope of a God who actively works in the profundities of human hearts.

Because God is alive, He could raise from the dead His precious Son, who – while fully God – took on human flesh to pay the pen-alty for human sinners. When the body of Jesus, the God-Man, lay in the tomb, God raised Him from the dead because God is alive and has all power. Never does God die and never can God be defeated; for He is living.

He is alive in an infinitely greater sense than we are alive, since He is the Author of life. And although His living seems too good to be true, Paul reassures the Thessalonians that our God is living *and* true. The reality of our living God corresponds exactly to what is said of Him. In other words, He lives up to His name in every way. While many people and powers claim to be many things, God actually is how awesome His Word portrays Him to be. He is true. He cannot fail. Though the idols, philosophies, and riches of first century Thessalonica could never meet the ultimate needs of humans, the living and true God could.

Since God is alive, He will be there in the most real way to carry me over the chasm of earthly death. I will die, but my God is forever and ever alive. As I trust Him, He will usher me into the next world when it is time. Because my God is alive, I will also live in glory.

May I submit to you that this same God – who is both alive and true – will change your life by redeeming you and walking with you both now and in eternity? Will you turn from all that falsely promises hope and, instead, turn to the living and true God? Even if you have already trusted God for salvation through Jesus Christ, make a renewed commitment to ponder the implications of serving a God who is both living and true.

Seeing the Unseen: Reflecting on a Winter Sunset

So we fix our eyes not on what is seen, but on what is unseen. For what is seen is temporary, but what is unseen is eternal.

II Corinthians 4:18 (NIV)

Seeing the unseen. Catching a glimpse of the eternal while stuck in the mundane flow of life. Paul had this in mind when he wrote in his second letter to the Corinthians, chapter four, verse eighteen, "So we fix our eyes not on what is seen, but on what is unseen. For what is seen is temporary, but what is unseen is eternal."

How do we fix our eyes on the unseen? Are not our eyes made for seeing what is visible? Yes, our eyes of flesh look at the visible, but our spiritual eyes are intended to behold the invisible. "By faith we understand that the universe was formed at God's command, so that what is seen was not made out of what was visible" (Hebrews 11:3). Aha, the essence of all we see in this world sprang from what we cannot see, God Himself. From God's viewpoint, training ourselves to look at the invisible is of utmost importance.

I took time one evening to look for quite some time at a beautiful winter sunset that caught my eye as I entered a room of my house. It was nearly completely dark outside, and so the sunset shone brightly through the window while the lights in the room were turned out. I had to stand in the darkened room to fully appreciate the blazing red glory resting just above the horizon and the bright, hopeful blue sky set atop the red brilliance. After observing for more than a few moments, I reached for the light switch so that I could return to my chore, the reason for entering the room in the first place. However, I was quite distracted by that light, as it obliterated my view of the beautiful sunset, making the window appear black compared to the brightness of the room.

Very quickly I once again reached for the switch – this time to turn off the light. I had to walk to the window and view that sunset

138

one more time, taking it into my heart as I drew a deep breath. And then I thought, "Only when this room and its immediate atmosphere right around me are dark can I appreciate the true beauty of the sunset in the distance." So it is. We cannot see the real beauty of God's work in our hearts and our world when we are focused intensely on our immediate needs, concerns, and selfish intentions. What are usually closest to our hearts are our own needs. When we finally "turn out the lights" on the seemingly pressing selfish wants and mundane busyness of life, we will be able to behold the eternal working of God Himself in our life and world in which we live.

The goal is for us to forget what we deem important and focus on what Jesus deems invaluable. We need to "turn off the lights" on the immediacy of self and turn our eyes to the invisible intentions of God in our lives. Maybe then, we will begin to see the beauty for which we are longing.

Let us aptly say, "Beauty – real beauty – is in the eye of the beholder of invisible things." To see the invisible, we have to sacrifice the self.

Thank you, Jesus, for that evening's winter sunset.

The Exo-Eso Effect

Therefore we do not lose heart, but though our outer man is decaying, yet our inner man is being renewed day by day. For momentary, light affliction is producing for us an eternal weight of glory far beyond all comparison.
II Corinthians 4:16-17

The concept of an inverse relationship is rather easy to understand: as one quantity increases, the other decreases. For example, as the price of a product increases, the quantity sold decreases. This simple mathematical relationship is brought to light in a wonderful piece of Scripture.

Do you realize that we are to avoid discouragement by recognizing a spiritual, inverse relationship? The apostle Paul tells us not to lose heart because "our outer man is decaying, yet our inner man is being renewed day by day" (II Corinthians 4:16). That's right, for every moment that our physical bodies are decaying, our inner spirit is being renewed and becoming more like Jesus!

I like to call this concept the "Exo-Eso Effect." The Greek root behind "outer man" is *exo* and the Greek root behind "inner man" is *eso*. What a hopeful, invigorating thought to know that as the outer shell of me wears away because of age and disease and hardship, the inner me is gaining new strength.

When Paul speaks of the outer man decaying, he is referring to the ruination of the body's vigor and strength; he is targeting the second law of thermodynamics as it applies to the wearing down of our physical bodies with age and affliction. None of us can avoid this process in this life, but we have proof positive that our condition will change in the next life. Residing within this body is a spirit that is growing in the grace and knowledge of Jesus Christ. Our spirit's growth and renewal day by day reminds us that our bodies which are in the process of dying will one day suddenly change too.

The Exo-Eso Effect is so plain to us, the people of God. Our bodies become tired, they ache, and they wear down. But, even as they do, we grow closer and closer to God. In fact, sometimes it is because we suffer tribulation in this physical body that we grow closer to God and are made more like Jesus! The inverse relationship is strong.

Paul went on to say that "momentary, light affliction is producing for us an eternal weight of glory far beyond all comparison" (II Corinthians 4:17). There it is again – the mysterious, inverse workings. My affliction is **momentary and light**. The glory produced is **eternal and weighty**! Hold onto that truth for dear life. We suffer now, and it can seem so heavy. However, compared to the eternal glory we shall enjoy, our affliction is nearly weightless. God promises that the good He is achieving through our commitment to Him is the heaviest of matters and lasts forever – literally. We simply cannot imagine how the trial of now could be so small compared to the glory of later, but that is because we have not experienced the vastness of eternity and perfection. We have to trust the One who holds eternity and perfection in the palm of His hand.

As we trust Him, we observe the Exo-Eso Effect in daily operation. My outer self is going downhill, but my inner self is growing in strength. This is not a problem for me, but an encouragement. My relationship with God through Jesus Christ is my hope. It is okay for this body to wear down and die, as long as my heart loves Jesus more and more. "Why," you ask? Because we know that "He who raised the Lord Jesus will raise us also with Jesus" (II Corinthians 4:14). In other words, even when the outer self finally does succumb to physical death, the inner relationship to the living God will overcome. The *eso* will overtake the *exo* on that glorious day when **"death is swallowed up in victory"** (I Corinthians 15:54).

For now, the Exo-Eso Effect is the outer self fading and the inner self growing. One day, the Exo-Eso Effect will culminate in a "new exo" that never wears away, never gets sick, and never grows tired. I'll take that hope while I make sure my "eso" is growing in Jesus.

Hope Found In Four Little Words

I know your deeds, that you are neither cold nor hot. I wish you were either one
or the other! So, because you are lukewarm – neither hot nor
cold – I am about to spit you out of my mouth.

Revelation 3:15-16 (NIV)

Half-hearted dedication stinks. We crave whole-heartedness – true devotion! Something in the soul of human beings longs for passion. Mediocrity is not attractive to us in any arena of life; and the reason is a simple one. The God who made us designed us for fervent worship. Mediocrity does not bring good results in sports, careers, relationships, studies, or any other area. It is repulsive in much the same way a mediocre relationship with God is abhorrent to Him. Our lives are designed to be all-consumed. We feel right when we are completely used up for God's sake. I am content when my efforts have been spent, my words have been spent, my emotions have been spent, my body has been spent, and my intellect has been spent for the purpose of Someone greater than I. That someone is the transcendent, personal God of the universe. I want to live a life of zeal for my God.

Perhaps this is why the words of Revelation 3:15-16 can sting so badly. Let us consider our lives – not in the broad sense – but in everyday moments of living. Let's think about our deeds: the way we arise in the morning, the look on our face when we meet someone before our first drink of coffee, the conversation we have over lunch, the way we approach housework, the way we approach our career, the goal we have in human encounters, the way we entertain ourselves, and a myriad of other actions. Are these things done rightly from a heart of passion that puts God's glory at the forefront? Or are our deeds sadly reflecting a heart that has lost its fervor for God's purposes in all things?

Picture a thermometer. The top line represents a red-hot relationship with Jesus Christ, the kind of relationship where His glory is your goal no matter the cost; you are consumed by an incomparable love for the Lord. The bottom line represents a quite dead, cold relationship with Jesus Christ. In fact, an affiliation this icy could hardly be considered a relationship. Now, on that thermometer, where would you place your relationship with God? At the very top line? At the very bottom? If you are like most people, you probably will not put it in either of those places, but somewhere in between. Perhaps you may even choose a level close to the top, but most likely – if we are honest –not at either extreme.

Given that assessment, let's now hear the words of Jesus in Revelation 3:15-16 (NIV), "I know your deeds, that you are neither cold nor hot. I wish you were either one or the other! So, because you are lukewarm – neither hot nor cold – I am about to spit you out of my mouth." Yikes! This does not sound good for people who are "in the middle somewhere." Jesus sees exactly where we are, and He is disgusted at a lukewarm heart. The Lord is so disgusted; He informs us that He would vomit us out of His mouth. Though I would not want to be a part of any regurgitation process, I most certainly would not want the Lord of my life to be repulsed by my heart's status. Sadly, I know there have been times in my life when I was on the receiving end of this horrifying rebuke.

My hope is found in four little words of verse sixteen, "I am *about* to." The New International Version seems to render the Greek word most accurately. The original word means "to be on the point of doing something; to intend; to have in mind." In other words, Jesus – because of our repugnant lukewarm status – is *ready* to vomit us out of His mouth, but *He has not yet done so.* This is tremendous! I deserve to be spit out, but Jesus is giving one window of opportunity with those four all-important words, "I am about to." Let the words roll through your mind. Say them aloud, "He is about to." He has not yet, but He certainly will *unless we turn around.* Thank God, we can!

Verse twenty of the same chapter informs us that Jesus is standing at the door of the lukewarm heart and knocking. He is taking the initiative; He believes we may just let Him in. If a man or woman opens the door, He will come in to have genuine, passionate relationship with that person. O blessed day, when Jesus comes in to make one who should be spit out into one who dines with the God of the universe!

Four life-changing words spoken by Jesus – "I am about to." I love those words. They bring forth a window of hope.

Is That Hole Really a Portal?

Not only so, but we also rejoice in our sufferings, because we know that
suffering produces perseverance; perseverance, character; and character, hope.
Romans 5:3-4 (NIV)

When disappointed to see a hole six inches in diameter near the top of a thick, evergreen bush in our front yard, I assumed the obvious defect was the result of the severe winter's heavy snow and huge icicles. As soon as the beautiful spring weather made obvious the unnatural cavity near the top of our bush, I became annoyed at the disfigurement. "What needless damage," I thought, as my mathematical mind longed for symmetry and perfection.

Just a few days later, my husband – knowing how I love birds – excitedly asked me if I had seen the baby robins. "Where?" I asked. You can guess his answer . . . "in the *bush* under the kitchen window." I rushed with my little nephews to see the oddly cute baby birds. How precious they were tucked away in the six-inch recess of our otherwise perfect bush. What a secure nest in which they rested, safely on the inner branches of the evergreen.

So, after all, the annoying hole in my bush is not just a hole, it is a portal . . . to new life. The dark cavity I thought a result of the random damage of winter months was a truly purposeful haven where life could begin. And so it is with our God of creation. He shows us that holes can be portals. He shows us that seemingly bad or needless things can – in all reality – be entrances to life. Romans 5:3-4 (NIV) says, "Not only so, but we also rejoice in our sufferings, because we know that suffering produces perseverance; perseverance, character; and character, hope." (NIV)

I can no more definitively explain how suffering results in hope than I can explain how robins construct sturdy nests with little beaks, or how God brings tiny birds out of eggs and makes them grow. But I know this, for people redeemed by God through

Jesus, behind every dark recess there is the victory of life. For the Christian, every abyss of suffering is truly a portal to perseverance, character, and – ultimately – hope. I have not known any suffering not accompanied by the need to persevere; I have known no trial that could not result in increased character, and I have known no heartache that the hope of Jesus could not soothe.

Our suffering is not an inconvenient hole in the otherwise orderliness of life; it is a portal to hope when viewed through the perspective of God. And, even now as I write this devotion, the baby robins chirp, "Amen!"

NOTES

Does Everything End With Us?

Halverson, Dean. 2003. *The Illustrated Guide to World Religions*. Bloomington, MN: Bethany House Publishers.

Vos, Matthew (2010/2011). "Kids These Days" in a World of Change. *Christian School Education*, 14 (1), 21-23.

Implications of Worry

Sprenger, M. (2005). How to teach so students remember. Alexandria, VA: Association for Supervision and Curriculum Development.

Willis, J. (2006). Research-based strategies to ignite student learning. Alexandria, VA: Association for Supervision and Curriculum Development.

Inaccessibly High Over "Indestructible" Anxiety

Samuelson, Robert, J. (2010, December 20). The flight from risk: recession's legacy stymies recovery. *Newsweek*, 20.

About the Author

Shelli Prindle is known for her passion, joy, and integrity. She clearly articulates biblical truth in a down-to-earth fashion that inspires people to practically apply it to their lives. As a writer, educator, and speaker, she engages the intellect and presents a message of true hope to audiences of all ages.

After receiving her bachelor of arts degree in mathematics and secondary education from Seton Hill University in Greensburg, Pennsylvania, Shelli spent more than a decade teaching math and Bible in Christian high schools in the Pittsburgh area. As a teacher, she devoted herself to the study of apologetics and Christian worldview. She obtained her master of arts degree in educational leadership from Crown College in Minnesota and has served as the principal/administrator of two Christian schools. Having achieved recognized leadership in Christian schooling, she has consulted with the Association of Christian Schools International (ACSI) to develop middle school leadership curriculum and has served as a seminar leader and conference speaker for ACSI since 2001.

In 2007, Shelli founded **Hope & Passion Ministries** as a vehicle through which to share her passion for God's Word and His people. **Sharing a Jesus-view of reality that produces true hope and passionate living** is the vision of Hope & Passion Ministries, Inc. This vision is realized as she teaches and speaks at churches, retreats, seminars, and conferences. While a writer of devotions, Shelli has also produced many original works including *Apologetics Activated!*, a ten hour practical primer on Christian apologetics and *The Heaven Event*, a half day presentation on the rock-solid nature of our eternal home.

If you would like more information about Hope & Passion Ministries or would like to consider Shelli to speak at your event, please visit the website at www.hopeandpassion.org or write to us at 126 Mount Pleasant Boulevard, Irwin, PA 15642.

Breinigsville, PA USA
14 April 2011
259750BV00003B/1/P